MANDY HAGER
HINDSIGHT

PIVOTAL MOMENTS IN NEW ZEALAND'S HISTORY

First published by OneTree House Ltd, New Zealand, 2019

© Mandy Hager, 2019

ISBN 978-0-9951065-4-3

All rights reserved. No part of this publication may be reproduced, stored in a retrieval system or transmitted in any form or by any means, electronic, mechanical, photocopying, recording or otherwise, without the prior permission of the publisher.

A catalogue record for this book is available from
the National Library of New Zealand

Design: Vasanti Unka
Edit: Dr Margaret Claire Dale
Research Intern: Alana Hawkes
Editorial and Design Assistance: Elizabeth Kirkby-McLeod

10 9 8 7 6 5 4 3 2   9 /1   0 1 2 3 /2

Printed in China

CONTENTS

Introduction 5

Women's Suffrage ------------------------------ 9

Springbok Tour ---------- 33

Dawn Raids ---------------------------------- 63

Rainbow Warrior -------- 84

Advice for researching in a 'Fake News' World -------------- 118

Kia ora,

The fascinating thing about digging back into our history is that it shows us who we were at certain points in time and how we've changed — or not changed — since that time. It shows us patterns of behaviour as well as the 'turning points' when something happens that changes peoples' lives, for good or bad, temporarily or permanently. These changes can be prompted by forces in the natural world, for instance earthquakes, volcanoes, storms or climate change. But there are human forces, too, which challenge the way we act as individuals in our community, society and in the wider world. And the way we approach any large scale change always involves political decisions, both individually and as a nation.

In fact, it's important to understand that in many ways *everything* is political. The decisions made by whoever represents us (and even the decision over who chooses who's allowed to represent us), shapes every aspect of our lives. The education system we are taught in, and what we are taught, is decided by those in power, as is our ability to go into tertiary education or take up an apprenticeship or have employment protections in place when we start work. The laws that bind us, the freedoms and civil liberties we are entitled to, our rights to decide our own fates, what we can watch and read, what we are free to say, who's allowed to live here, whether we'll ever afford to buy a house, who we can marry, our rights to privacy, all these things and many more are affected by the values and policies of the people who represent us in our parliament. In healthy democracies, this also means the values of the people who elect their representatives affect the decisions of politicians.

In the case of all four pivotal moments explored in this book, change was led by ordinary people who felt the values driving our laws and actions needed an adjustment; ordinary people who reached out to other like-minded people and joined forces to create change. This book is about that people power, and maps the pathways many courageous groups took to bring about desired changes — changes that, in the long run, have benefited us all.

INTRODUCTION

The late cultural anthropologist Margaret Mead said: *Never doubt that a small group of thoughtful, committed citizens can change the world; indeed, it's the only thing that ever has.* The case studies in this book certainly provide good evidence to support this claim. In every chapter, we meet people who risked their positions, freedoms and, sometimes, even their lives, to bring about improvements to their own and others' human rights. These people all showed a determination to fight on someone else's behalf, not only thinking about themselves. This ability to consider the plight of others with empathy and compassion, not merely self-interest, is something I urge you to take away from reading this. Put yourself into the hearts and minds of those whose human rights were being denied or their safety threatened. Think about how you would have reacted and ask yourself why? Do your views and values on each issue come from having thought them through, seeking out both sides of the argument so you can make an informed choice? Or do you just go along with the thinking of the current crowd? Or rely on only one news source, possibly with its own conscious or unconscious bias? Take time to recognise how your own life has been enhanced by the gutsy efforts of the many people represented in these pages. Would you be prepared to do the same?

It's been cheering to research the moments explored in this book. Despite all the shocking injustices, bigotry and brutality explored here, what most stands out is the steadfast spirit of those who fought for change, reminding me of everything that is decent and admirable in human nature. These topics are also all personal to me. I lived through three of them, actively participated in two, and saw my mother still having to battle for basic women's rights that my daughter now takes for granted — and which millions of women alive today still don't possess.

I have presented the facts as thoroughly as I can, taking specific note of the human rights implications for each moment. I've focussed on the four P's: the People (who was involved and why), the Politics (including how societies work and what changed at a political level), the differing Perspectives of the time, and the Payoff (short and long-terms consequences). You'll notice that the chapter on the 1981 Springbok Tour comes before the Dawn Raids, even though the Dawn Raids took place first. I've done this because I think the racism discussed in the Springbok Tour chapter reflects many of the same issues seen in the times of the Dawn Raids, just on a bigger scale. And I want you to think about the implications of the steady erosion of laws that allowed the apartheid system to operate, and to keep this in mind as you look at how we teetered on the edge of equally ugly racism.

It's also important to remember that, in all these social movements, there were people who chose *not* to participate; who either didn't care enough to act, didn't agree, or chose to look the other way.

When there is a big movement unfolding around us, choosing to stay out of it is taking a position too. And that's okay, so long as we all understand that the choices we make in life are, at least in part, shaped by our upbringing and the values held up as important in our society — and that we also have the choice to change our minds when presented with more compelling evidence.

In much the same way, what I've chosen to present here as fact and evidence, and the emphasis I've placed on certain events and actions, is shaped by *my* values. It's important you keep this in mind.

Another writer may have chosen a whole different set of sources for their information and highlighted a whole set of completely different people, events and points of view. What another writer feels is important, for a proper understanding of our history may be completely different. Some writers of non-fiction claim that they approach the material in a totally neutral way, providing unbiased balance to each issue, but even this stance is value-driven; everything included is still selected by a person with a point of view. What and who is omitted from history is as much a political act as what is told. For instance, throughout this project I've noticed a distinct lack of women's voices included in much of the historic narrative. Why do you think this might be?

With accusations flying around today about 'fake news' — and such a huge flood of information and opinion available on the internet — it's vitally important that *you* approach any information (including this book) with a few crucial questions ringing in your head:

- Who is saying this? What is their intention? What are their motives? Is this someone whose opinions I trust?
- Who does this information (and its underlying point of view) benefit? Is it designed to silence critics, spread false information, back up dubious claims? Examples might include such things as a site that publishes articles on climate change denial, funded by the fossil fuel industry, or a political party trying to 'spin' the truth, or a white supremacist trying to influence the way you feel about refugees and migrants.
- What is the real source of this information? It's always worth following back through articles and checking references. Do the primary sources seem trustworthy and traceable? Wikipedia is an excellent example of a site that, at its best, contains a wealth of well-researched information (if you can verify the sources) while, at its worst, is a biased load of (bleep!) and totally untrue!
- Does any data (charts, statistics etc) come from a credible source? Has it been presented in such a way as to influence the way you read and interpret it?
- Does this information contain unconscious bias? This refers to a bias that a writer is unaware of and which happens outside of their control. It is a bias that happens automatically and is triggered by our brain making quick judgements and assessments of people and situations, influenced by our background, cultural environment and personal experiences. As a Pākehā writer, for instance, I may think that I am fairly representing other races but might not be aware that my 'white privilege' is showing. This can also be the case with 'male privilege' or

'economic privilege'. For example, with this book, as I mentioned earlier, I'm absolutely privileging my belief in equality and human rights, even when I'm not consciously doing so. This doesn't necessarily make the information any less relevant, but it is important that you know so you can decide whether this is acceptable or not. And it is equally important to test your own unconscious biases and see them for what they are. We all have them. We also all have the power to readjust our blinkers and see the world through 'others' eyes, in order to truly 'see' our common humanity. Our human community.

With these questions in mind, I invite you to enter into the worlds of four very important moments in our history. It's not meant to be the definitive word on each subject, space prevents that, but an introduction, a start. I've included as many sources and links to additional information as I could, and hope this may inspire you to look into them further. Most of the material is sourced from the internet, in order that you can easily go online to read each reference in full and check the sources for yourself, if you wish to dig deeper. I recommend it!

I also urge you to apply these same rigorous thinking tools to the issues currently taking place. As I write this introduction, we, as a country, have just faced another huge test of our humanity and values as a result of the terrorist attack on innocent people in Christchurch. It brought the country together for several weeks, with cries of 'this is not us' and 'we are one.' This open-hearted response shows us what we're capable of: a society where *every* person is valued, no matter their colour, culture or belief. But as the weeks have slipped by since, that message has been diluted by those with vested interests, especially those who have a preconceived idea of who 'we' are and what 'we' aspire to be. Before you jump on any bandwagon of thought, drill back down to your first gut response: that we should be operating from a place of inclusiveness and love for all. Become one of Margaret Mead's *thoughtful and committed citizens*; be, as Mahatma Gandhi encouraged, *the change you wish to see in the world.*

In 2016 I published a book about a woman who had lived in 12th century France. In researching about her life, I had to learn all about the politics and attitudes of the time, to understand how she and the people around her acted and thought, in order to make sense of what happened to her. Having this historical context hugely changed my understanding about some of the things she experienced and why. What really amazed me, was how much the underlying pressures in her world were like our own — and how little we have changed. Winston Churchill said: *"Those that fail to learn from history, are doomed to repeat it."* I think, for me, the best reason for learning more about our past is that history can help us understand what brought us here — and also gives us an opportunity to learn from it, and maybe, just maybe, stop repeating the mistakes of our past.

Are you up for it?

Mandy Hager
May 2019

EXTRAORDINARY WOMEN

THE STORY OF NEW ZEALAND WOMEN'S RIGHT TO VOTE

We often take our freedoms for granted — perhaps aware that our small nation was the first to legislate for women's **franchise,** but knowing little of the long, hard fight that led to this historic win, or the people to whom we owe such a debt. In the 21st century, it may be hard to imagine what it was like for Aotearoa/New Zealand's early women: denied the vote, with limited rights to decide their own fate, and publicly scorned if they dared to speak out against the men who ruled almost every aspect of their lives.

The story of Aotearoa/New Zealand women's voting rights not only shines a light onto the issue of **gender equality,** but also provides a window into the bigger democratic story, that of **universal suffrage,** where every citizen of a country over a certain age is allowed to vote in free and fair elections. In many countries, even once women's suffrage was granted, some sections of society were still unable to vote if they came from certain classes or races. In other cases, such as Sweden in the 18th century, women were granted the right to vote, only to have this decision overturned four years later and their full voting rights not finally restored until 1919. This is a good reminder that the state of our democratic rights requires constant checks to prevent back-peddling and erosion.

It's worth noting that there are still countries where voting is the privilege of a select few, or where the standards of freedom to vote in lawfully-run elections fall short, corrupting the democratic process.

Even today, Aotearoa/New Zealanders who are sentenced to prison are not entitled to enrol and vote, nor are those who have been in a psychiatric hospital for more than three years after being charged with a criminal offence. A New Zealand citizen who has not been in New Zealand within the last three years cannot enrol and vote either, nor can any permanent residents who have not been in the country within the last twelve months prior to an election.

WOMEN VOTE FOR THE FIRST TIME AT A POLLING STATION IN THE TINY SOUTH OTAGO SETTLEMENT OF TAHAKOPA ON 28 NOVEMBER 1893.

Mary Wollstonecraft:
"I shall first consider women in the grand light of human creatures, who, in common with men, are placed on this earth to unfold their faculties."

MARY WOLLSTONECRAFT

THE DEBRIEF
Do you know which countries still restrict women or other groups from their elections? The website 'The Debrief' has a Pg called *Here Are The Countries Where It's Still Really Difficult For Women To Vote* **Take a look online!**

THE BEGINNINGS OF THE WOMEN'S RIGHTS MOVEMENT

Many credit Englishwoman Mary Wollstonecraft (1797 – 1851) with the first modern expression of feminist ideas. Inspired by the French Revolution, in 1792 she wrote a book called *A Vindication of the Rights of Women,* calling for equal rights for women, including proper education. Before this, books had been written arguing for improvements in female education, but often the goal was merely to better prepare women for their role as companions for men. In contrast, Wollstonecraft criticised women's education: *"I attribute [these problems] to a false system of education, gathered from the books written on this subject by men, who, considering females rather as women than human creatures, have been more anxious to make them alluring mistresses than affectionate wives and rational mothers… the civilised women of this present century, with a few exceptions, are only anxious to inspire love, when they ought to cherish a nobler ambition, and by their abilities and virtues exact respect."*[1]

Her book called for equal education provided by the State, offered to both sexes together. She protested against the idea that women were merely playthings for men, claiming that intellectual companionship was the chief source of happiness in marriage.

It was to be nearly 100 years later that the fight for women's rights heated up in colonial New Zealand, inspired by other thinkers from Britain and the United States. Of particular influence at the time was the British philosopher John Stuart Mills, who, in his essay *The Subjection of Women* (1869), said: 'In early times, the great majority of the male sex were slaves, as well as the whole of the female. And many ages elapsed, some of them ages of high cultivation, before any thinker was bold enough to *question the rightfulness, and the absolute social necessity, either of the one slavery or of the other.'*

His wife, Harriet Taylor Mills, was also a significant influence. Her essay, *'The Enfranchisement of Women'* (1851), is considered one of her most important works, although it was published under her husband's name. The essay argued that women should be given access to the same jobs as men, and that they should not have to live in 'separate spheres' — views thought even more radical than those of Mills himself. English woman Barbara Bodichon's campaign for married women's rights also prompted much discussion. Overseas speakers often travelled to Aotearoa/New Zealand to spread these radically modern thoughts.

In this new colony, such ideas found fertile ground. Many settler women worked alongside men, struggling to set up and maintain homes. These women were often deserted or left in charge of properties and family (and sometimes businesses) while their husbands sought riches in the coal mines or gold and kauri fields.

Improved educational opportunities for Aotearoa/New Zealand's women also played an important role. Unlike many of the countries they had emigrated from, secondary schools for girls were opened in Aotearoa/New Zealand during the 1870s and women were admitted into universities from 1871.

With better education, Aotearoa/New Zealand women were able to enter the workforce, most as teachers, but others as doctors, lawyers and journalists, or self-employed businesswomen. By the late 1880s, over seven hundred women who couldn't vote employed men who could!

KEYWORDS

Colony: A geographical area politically controlled by a distant country, the 'homeland'.

Freeholders: Owners of land or property who have the freedom to dispose of it at will.

Gender Equality: The state of being equal, especially in status, rights, or opportunities for both women and men.

Householders: The head of a household, although not necessarily owning the house.

Leaseholders: Those who lease land or property, with rights to use but not to own or sell.

Plural voting: The ability to vote in more than one district.

Representation: Actions taken on behalf of a chosen group of people by those elected to Parliament.

Suffrage: The right to vote (also referred to as franchise.)

Temperance: Abstinence (refraining) from alcoholic drink.

DID YOU KNOW?

The first female university graduate in Aotearoa/New Zealand was Kate Edgar in 1877. She was also the first woman to gain a Bachelor of Arts degree in the British Empire. Appointed to teach at Christchurch Girls' High School, she continued to study and was capped with a Master of Arts degree from Canterbury College in 1882

KATE EDGAR

PRE 1893 (WOMEN'S SUFFRAGE) NEW ZEALAND VOTING RIGHTS

1853: The first Aotearoa/New Zealand election. Although considered liberal for its time, the first parliamentary election reflected British traditions, and all women were excluded, along with 'aliens' (non-British subjects), inmates of prisons and asylums, those newly immigrated who had lived in a district less than six months, and those workers such as farm labourers, seafarers and bushmen, who rarely owned property. Most Māori men were also excluded, despite being British subjects, as the majority of their land was owned communally and they didn't possess individual titles granted by the Crown. This situation was welcomed by most settlers, who, coming from white-dominated societies, unfairly claimed that Māori were not yet capable of being given such an important responsibility. Even so, around 100 Māori (mostly tribal leaders who owned houses in or around European settlements) did vote in the first election.

1860: Parliament extends the right to vote to gold miners, many of whom did not meet the property requirement. This move was in response to violent protests erupting on the goldfields of Australia over similar issues. By giving Aotearoa/New Zealand gold miners the right to vote the government hoped to avoid similar outbursts here. The legislation allowed any male British subject over 21 years of age who held a miner's right (a £1 annual licence) to vote in his local electorate without having to enrol. This did not, however, extend to the 2,000 Chinese gold miners who had travelled here by 1869 (5,000 by 1881).

1863: Voting extended to holders of 'goldfield business licences', which cost £5 per year. This move, which created special 'goldfield seats' in Otago and Westland, boosted the 41,500 registered electors by an additional 20,000 miners.

1867: The Māori Representation Act saw the creation of four specially targeted Māori seats — three in the North Island and one for the entire South island. To get around the problem of communal land ownership, Māori men over the age of 21 were granted the universal right to vote (12 years before all Pākehā men). Proposed initially as a temporary solution, in 1876 the seats were confirmed as permanent. While this sounds like a big step forwards, if the allocation of seats had been based on population numbers at the time, Māori would have been entitled to 15 seats (while Pākehā at the time had 72). The issue of Māori-specific seats remains in dispute to this day.

TIMELINE

1870: Adoption of secret ballots to replace the previous verbal voting system. This reinforced the idea that voting was an individual right and choice rather than a privilege.

1875: Women ratepayers granted rights to vote in local body elections. Already granted previously to women in Otago and Nelson, this right was now extended to all provinces, the first step on the path to full voting rights.

1876: The Lodgers' Franchise Act was passed, extending the vote to young tradesmen and clerks who lived in boarding houses. It was to prove confusing and difficult to enforce.

1879: Vote granted to all adult European men who had been resident in a Aotearoa/New Zealand electorate for 12 months or more. Freeholder's rights and plural voting were retained, although the property value threshold was reduced to £25. This was to have a huge impact on the following 1881 election, where 91% of the 82,271 registered voters were adult Pākehā men and for the first time 'working men', not only the wealthy colonial elite, were elected.

19 September 1893: The new Electoral Act makes Aotearoa/New Zealand the first self-governing country in the world to *grant the right to vote to all adult women*, decades before other democratic countries. British women had to wait until 1918 and the entire population of American women were not granted the vote until 1920.

THE LONG JOURNEY TO THE 1893 ELECTORAL ACT:

"The news is being flashed far and wide, and before our earth has revolved on her axis every civilized community within the reach of the electric wires will have received the tidings that civic freedom has been granted to the women of New Zealand…"
Kate Sheppard in a statement after the New Zealand legislature gave women the right to vote (September 1893)

The bravery of the many women who spoke out and suffered public abuse and backlash to push for their voting rights makes for inspiring reading. At the time, 'respectable' women were expected to bend to the will of their husbands, keep house and raise families. Those who did speak out often did so against the wishes of their husbands, with some early supporters expressing their views under assumed names (rather than risk using their own.) The journey to women's suffrage in Aotearoa/New Zealand was undertaken by a series of exceptional women who fought for the rights of all women, not only an elite few.

THE ORIGINAL PETITION ON DISPLAY
AS PHOTOGRAPHED BY DOM POST.

NOTICE TO EPICENE WOMEN.

ELECTIONEERING WOMEN

ARE REQUESTED NOT TO CALL HERE.

They are recommended to go home, to look after their children, cook their husband's dinners, empty the slops, and generally attend to the domestic affairs for which Nature designed them.

By taking this advice they will gain the respect of all right-minded people—an end not to be attained by unsexing themselves and meddling in masculine concerns of which they are profoundly ignorant.

HENRY WRIGHT.

103, Mein Street,
Wellington.

SUFFRAGE MILESTONES #2

1869: Mary Ann Müller ('Femmina') wrote 'An appeal to the men of New Zealand', advocating votes for women.

1871: Mary Colclough ('Polly Plum') gave her first public lecture on the rights of women, including their right to vote. Letters to and from 'Polly Plum' appeared in the New Zealand Herald in 1871.

1874: J.C. Andrew in the House of Representatives urged that women be enfranchised.

1878: Robert Stout unsuccessfully proposed in his Electoral Bill that women ratepayers be eligible to vote for and be elected as members of the House of Representatives.

1879: The government's Qualification of Electors Bill was amended to give women property owners the vote, but parliamentarians who wanted all women to be enfranchised joined with those who opposed the reform to defeat the amendment.

1880: A Women's Franchise Bill introduced by James Wallis lapsed after its first reading.

1881: Another Women's Franchise Bill introduced by Wallis was withdrawn before its second reading.

1885: The New Zealand Women's Christian Temperance Union (WCTU) was established following the visit of American temperance campaigner Mary Leavitt; by February 1886 there were 15 branches.

1886: At its first annual convention in Wellington, presided over by Anne Ward, the WCTU resolved to work for women's suffrage. Kate Sheppard took up the role of national superintendent of their franchise and legislation department.

1887: Two petitions requesting the franchise signed by some 350 women were presented to the House of Representatives. A Women's Suffrage Bill to enfranchise women and give them the right to sit in Parliament was introduced by Julius Vogel but withdrawn at the committee stage.

1888: Two petitions asking for the enfranchisement of women signed by around 800 women were presented to the Legislative Council.

1889: The Tailoresses' Union of Aotearoa/New Zealand was established in Dunedin; many of its members, including the vice-president, Harriet Morison, were active in the suffrage campaign.

1890: A Women's Franchise Bill introduced by Sir John Hall late in the parliamentary session lapsed, in spite of majority support, because there was no time to consider it. Hall then moved an amendment to the Electoral Bill to enfranchise women, but this was defeated.

1891: Eight petitions asking for the franchise signed by more than 9,000 women were presented to the House of Representatives. A Female Suffrage Bill introduced by Hall received majority support in the House of Representatives but was narrowly defeated in the Legislative Council.

1892: The Women's Franchise League was established first in Dunedin and later elsewhere. Six petitions asking for the franchise signed by more than 19,000 women were presented to the House of Representatives. The Electoral Bill, introduced by John Ballance, provided for the enfranchisement of all women. Controversy over an impractical postal vote amendment caused its abandonment.

1893: Thirteen petitions requesting that the franchise be conferred on women were signed by nearly 32,000 women, compiled and presented to the House of Representatives. Meri Te Tai Mangakāhia addressed the Māori parliament to ask that Māori women be allowed to vote for and become members of that body, but the matter lapsed. A Women's Suffrage Bill was introduced by Hall in June but withdrawn in October after it was overtaken by the Electoral Act. An Electoral Bill containing provision for women's suffrage was introduced by Richard Seddon in June. During debate, there was majority support for the enfranchisement of Māori as well as Pākehā women. The bill was passed by the Legislative Council on 8 September (after last-minute changes of allegiance) and consented to by the Governor on 19 September. The Electoral Act 1893 gave all women in Aotearoa/New Zealand the right to vote. On 29 November, the day after the general election, Elizabeth Yates was elected mayor of the borough of Onehunga – the first woman in the British Empire to hold such an office.

1919: The Women's Parliamentary Rights Act gave women the right to stand for Parliament. Three women contested seats at the 1919 general election, but none were successful.

1933: The Labour Party's Elizabeth McCombs became the first female Member of Parliament (MP), winning a by-election in the Lyttelton seat following the death of her husband, MP James McCombs.

MARY ANN MÜLLER

'Our women are brave and strong, with an amount of self-reliance and freedom from conventionalities eminently calculated to form a great nation. Give them scope. At present their grasp and power of mind is 'cribbed, cabined, and confined' to one narrow groove. It is weakened and famished by disuse, and only a close observer can detect the latent force, the unspent energy lying dormant in many seemingly ordinary characters.'
From 'An Appeal to the Men of New Zealand. 1869'.

MEET THE SUFFRAGISTS:

One of the earliest public activists was English-born Nelson woman **Mary Ann Müller**, who came to Aotearoa/New Zealand with two of her three children and was believed to have left behind her first husband 'on account of his cruelty.' [3] After meeting the English women's rights advocate, Maria Rye, during her visit here in 1864, Müller began to write articles in the Nelson Examiner under the pen name '**Fémmina**', disguising her identity because her second husband did not approve of her feminist views. These articles were widely distributed and soon travelled far beyond Nelson.

In 1869 Müller wrote the first pamphlet on the woman's vote to be published in Aotearoa/New Zealand, marking the start of the suffrage movement here. *An Appeal to the Men of New Zealand* argued that women should not be discriminated against in law or politics because of their gender, and had just as much entitlement to the vote as men. She emphasised women couldn't fully contribute to the progress of the nation without political rights. *'How long'*, she asked, *'are women to remain a wholly unrepresented body of the people?'* She implored men to answer the call and fight for electoral reform and included a special plea to parliamentarians: *'Women's eyes turn in hope – nay trust – on some leading spirits who will not fail them.'*

'Let the laws be fitted to the people and times. Do you still persecute for religious opinions? Do you still burn for witchcraft? Why, when the broad road of progress is cleared for so many human beings, is the juggernaut car of prejudice still to be driven on, crushing the crowds of helpless women beneath its wheels?'
Mary Müller writing as 'Fémmina' in her 1869 pamphlet 'An Appeal to the Men of New Zealand.'

She sent a copy of her pamphlet to John Stuart Mill in 1870 and received a congratulatory letter back from him, urging her to form a committee to fight for the vote. Although she couldn't do this publicly, she did meet with politicians, notably Alfred Saunders and William Fox, [#4] who took up the cause on women's behalf, as did Sir George Grey, Sir Julius Vogel, Sir John Hall and Sir Robert Stout.

Another woman who took on the battle around this time was teacher **Mary Colclough**, more famously known by her pen name '**Polly Plum**'. Not only did she take on the opposition through letters in local newspapers, but she also gave public lectures in Auckland, Thames, Ngaruawahia and Hamilton – a remarkable action for a woman at that time. She called for temperance (the banning of alcohol) and the improved treatment of women prisoners and prostitutes (and involved herself in their practical rehabilitation). But, above all, she campaigned for women's rights. Her profile in the Dictionary of New Zealand Biography says:

She argued that women were entitled to education, careers and the vote. In her opinion the role of wife and mother was very important but it was absurd to educate girls purely for domestic life. As single women, widows, or wives of improvident husbands, many would have to support themselves. Self-reliance and self-help were the keys. There should be no legal barrier to women rising as high in the world as their talents would take them. Finally, justice demanded that women should not be subject to laws they had no part in making. [#5]

Want to dig down into a little more research yourself?

Check out the biographies of other women and men who played a crucial part in Aotearoa/New Zealand's suffrage movement. They include: Lily Atkinson, John Balance, Margaret Bullock, Dulcie Cabot, Elizabeth Caradus, Amey Daldy, Learmonth Dalrymple, Kate Edgar, Catherine Fulton, William Fox, George Grey, Edith Grossmann, John Hall, Marion Hatton, Christina Henderson, Niniwa Heremaia, Emily Hill, Nettie Florence Keller, Lily Kirk, Colin Stuart Lovell-Smith, Rata Alice Lovell-Smith, Jessie Mackay, Mackay John Scobie Mackenzie, Meri Te Tai Mangakahia, Isabella May, Harriet Morison, Helen Lyster Nicol, Iriaka Matiu Rātana, Lizzie Rattray, Magdalene Stuart Reeves, Rachel Reynolds, Alfred Saunders, Annie Schnackenberg, Richard John Seddon, Margaret Home Siewright, Robert Stout, Julius Vogel, James Wallis, Anne Ward, Elizabeth Yates. You'll find many here at:

https://teara.govt.nz or https://nzhistory.govt.nz/

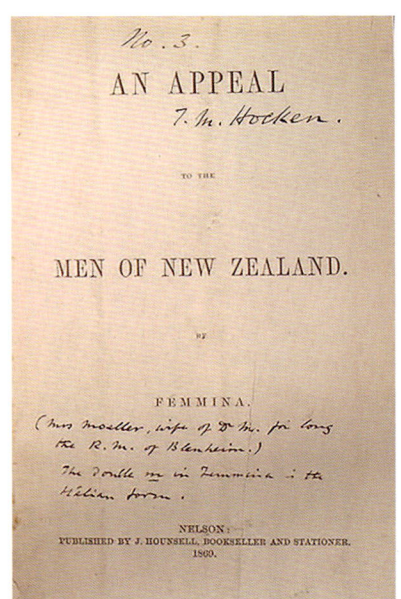

COVER OF THE ORIGINAL 1869 PAMPHLET, HELD AT HOCKEN LIBRARY, DUNEDIN.

'Is it right that your mother, your sister… should be classed with criminals and lunatics…? Is it right that while the gambler, the drunkard, and even the wife-beater has a vote, earnest, educated and refined women are denied it?… Is it right… that a mother… should be thought unworthy of a vote that is freely given to the blasphemer, the liar, the seducer, and the profligate? Is it right?' Kate Sheppard 1892

Do you know the meaning of the white camellia?

These flowers were given to members of Parliament who supported the suffrage bill, and have since become a symbol of the fight for women's suffrage. In the Christchurch Botanical Gardens a memorial walk dedicated to Sheppard is lined with white camellias.

KATE SHEPPARD — THE ENDURING FACE OF THE MOVEMENT

The most well-known and celebrated advocate for women's suffrage in Aotearoa/New Zealand is Kate Sheppard, whose face today graces our ten dollar note and fifty cent stamp. Born Catherine Wilson Malcolm in Liverpool, England in 1847, she was said to be highly intelligent, and gained an excellent education in the sciences, arts and law before she travelled to Aotearoa/New Zealand in 1868 with her mother and two brothers, after the death of her father in 1862. The family settled in Christchurch, where she met and married Walter Sheppard at the age of 24 and had a son (Douglas) in 1880.

An active member of the Trinity Congregational Church, she volunteered as secretary of the Ladies Association and, along with other members of her family, became involved in temperance (anti-alcohol) work. After a visit in 1885 by Mary Leavitt, a delegate of the Woman's Christian Temperance Union of the USA, Kate became one of the founding members of the New Zealand Women's Christian Temperance Union (WCTU) and went on to become the Union's national superintendent of the franchise and legislation department.

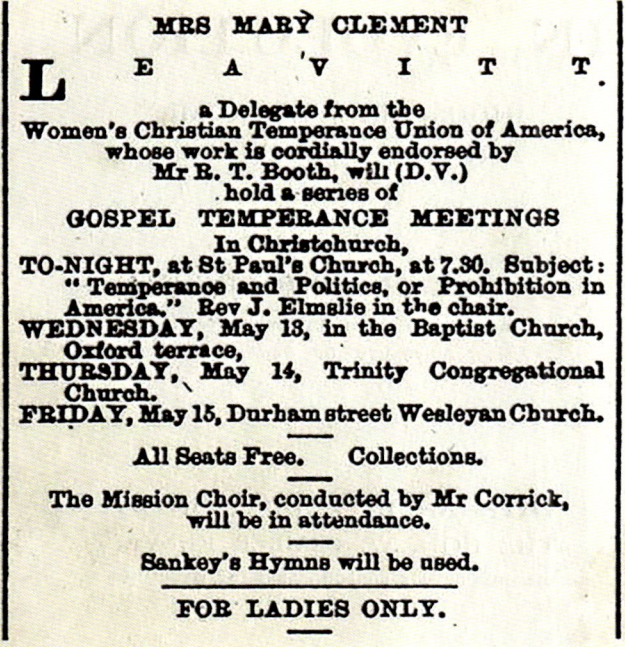

MEETING NOTICE FROM LYTTELTON TIMES, 12 MAY 1885. AFTER MARY LEAVITT'S VISIT, KATE SHEPPARD BECAME A FOUNDING MEMBER OF THE NEW ZEALAND WOMEN'S CHRISTIAN TEMPERANCE UNION.

What was the New Zealand Women's Christian Temperance Union (NZWCTU)?

Aotearoa/New Zealand's first national women's organisation, members were united by a concern over the damage done to families by alcohol abuse. Within seven months of being founded in 1885, the first 10 branches had been formed. They were involved in all matters affecting women, not only temperance, although they lobbied hard to prevent the sale of alcohol to minors (those under 21) and children, and to end the mistreatment of barmaids. As well as this, they initiated:
- classes in healthy clothing, food, and diets for the sick;
- preschool centres, run by WCTU volunteers;
- support to those fighting for better conditions for women in the workplace, and those considered 'fallen women' (pregnant outside marriage or prostitutes etc) were helped to find jobs and homes.

They also ran soup kitchens and raised funds for a night shelter for the homeless during the 1880s economic depression, and set up 'prison-gate missions' to meet and support newly released prisoners until they were back on their feet.

Alongside this, they campaigned for clinics to treat sexually transmitted diseases and to repeal the Contagious Diseases Act, which was used to forcibly examine and treat any woman suspected of being a prostitute.

Perhaps most importantly, they worked tirelessly, under the leadership of Kate Sheppard, to get women the right to vote.

Motivated by strong social justice and humanitarian principles, Kate co-ordinated and encouraged all the local temperance unions, distributed pamphlets, wrote letters to newspapers and lobbied politicians and other suffrage supporters, spoke at public meetings and inspired debate within the WCTU and other like-minded organisations. She believed that *'all that separates, whether of race, class, creed or sex, is inhuman, and must be overcome'*. Sheppard was frustrated that women, excluded from the right to cast a vote, had been put in the same category as children, lunatics and criminals.

When the 1875 Act gave all women ratepayers the right to vote in municipal (local body) elections, this was seen as an indication of growing support for women's rights. But despite the backing of a number of Aotearoa/New Zealand's leading male politicians (including John Hall, Robert Stout, Julius Vogel, William Fox and John Ballance) parliamentary bills or amendments designed to give women (or at the least, women ratepayers) the vote in general elections, were defeated in 1878, 1879, and 1887.

Under Kate's energetic leadership, the WCTU took the first of three key petitions to Parliament in 1891, which had over 9,000 signatures combined in eight separate regional petitions. When this had no effect, six further petitions were signed by more than 19,000 women. Again, they were ignored. But more and more franchise leagues were being set up around the country, reaching out to the smaller centres too, and in 1893 the largest combined petition yet was presented to Parliament, with nearly 32,000 signatures from thirteen regional petitions.

By now this small group of 600 women in the WCTU had pushed the issue of franchise firmly into the public eye. Thanks to this great effort, they gained so much support that their demands could no longer be dismissed. Sir John Hall put forward a bill for women's suffrage and managed to get it passed by Parliament's lower house; all they needed now was for the bill to be passed by the Legislative Council. The women were ecstatic.

But, just as their dream was about to come true, the premier, John Balance, who had supported their cause, suddenly died. An opponent of women's suffrage, Richard John Seddon, was named the new premier. Seddon was relying on his Legislative Council to defeat the bill and, just to make sure, appointed twelve new members to the Council, of whom at least half were known to oppose women's suffrage. However, in his own attempts to stop the bill passing, he so enraged two of the members he'd put pressure on that they decided to vote in support, and the bill was passed.

Even then, the fight was still not quite over. Some members of the Council now tried to convince the new Governor, Lord Glasgow, not to sign the bill into law. The suffragists fired back into action, sending telegrams and rallying on the 8th of September to deliver all members of Parliament who had supported women's suffrage a white camellia, and those who opposed it a red camellia, in order to clearly highlight each member's position. To Seddon's disappointment, the Governor signed the bill.

On 19 September 1893, the Electoral Act 1893 gave women the vote. When speaking about it afterwards, although jubilant, Kate Sheppard said:

'It does not seem a great thing to be thankful for, that the gentlemen who confirm the laws which render women liable to taxation and penal servitude have declared us to be "persons"… We are glad and proud to think that even in so conservative a body as the Legislative Council there is a majority of men who are guided by the principles of reason and justice, who desire to see their womenkind treated as reasonable beings, and who have triumphed over prejudice, narrow-mindedness and selfishness.'

Just ten weeks later, in the November, Aotearoa/New Zealand's women participated in the general election for the first time. The WCTU once again activated their networks right around the country, encouraging women of all classes to enrol and vote. As a result of their efforts, 65% of eligible women used their right to vote, with 90,290 women casting their votes (85% of the total number of registered women, as opposed to just under 70% of registered men). With this level of participation, the well-worn argument that only a handful of women actually desired the power to vote was finally put to rest.

ELECTION DAY IN NEW PLYMOUTH, 1893

MĀORI WOMEN AND THE VOTE

While settler women had sexism and class discrimination to contend with, the Māori women of Aotearoa/New Zealand had the added burden of racist colonial attitudes in their fight to gain the right to vote. They were actively involved in supporting the WCTU, while also seeking the right to vote and stand for seats in Te Kotahitanga, the Māori Parliament. Such was their determination and hard work, that, by the end of the century, they saw both these goals achieved. Their national collective, Ngā Komiti Wāhine, continued to be a political voice even after the closure of the Māori Parliament in 1902.

MEET THREE OF THESE WĀHINE TOA:

MERI TE TAI MANGAKĀHIA (1868 – 1920)

Meri Te Tai Mangakāhia (Ngāti Te Reinga, Ngāti Manawa and Te Kaitutae) studied at St Mary's Convent, Auckland, and in the late 1880s or early 1890s became the third wife of Hamiora Mangakāhia, an assessor in the Native Land Court. He attended the meeting in the Bay of Islands in 1889 when Te Kotahitanga, the Māori Parliament movement, formally began. He was elected as premier of the Kotahitanga Parliament in 1892. Mother of four children (including Mabel, thought to have been the first Māori to receive a postgraduate diploma in public health nursing in 1939), Meri Te Tai became a strong supporter of the women's suffrage movement and, in May 1893, initiated a motion in the Kotahitanga Parliament that asked for women to be granted the right to help select its members. Later that day she addressed the Parliament — the first woman on record to have done so [#6] — requesting not only that Māori women be given the vote, but also be granted the right to sit in the Māori Parliament. She ended her plea with the words:

"I pray to this gathering that women members be appointed. Perhaps by this course of action we may be satisfied concerning the many issues affecting us and our land. Perhaps the Queen may listen to the petitions if they are presented by her Māori sisters, since she is a woman as well."
Meri Te Tai Mangakāhia

NINIWA HEREMAIA OR NINIWA-I-TE-RANGI (1854 – 1929)

Niniwa-i-te-rangi (Ngāti Kahungunu) was born at Oroi, on the east coast of Wairarapa, the eldest surviving daughter of Heremaia Tamaihotua, the leading chief of Ngāti Hikawera of Ngāti Kahungunu. Her natural ability as a speaker, along with her knowledge of whakapapa and tradition, saw her win significant battles in the Native Land Court. A leader among Wairarapa Māori, she supported the women's rights movement and was involved in hosting the Kotahitanga Parliament when it met at Pāpāwai in 1897 and 1898. Later she took an editorial role in setting up the Maori-language

MERI TE TAI MANGAKĀHIA

newspapers *Te Puke ki Hikurangi* and *Te Tiupiri*. In 1898 she was the only woman who gave evidence to Parliament's Native Affairs Committee inquiry into Māori land legislation. In 1904 Niniwa sponsored the production of the *Maori Record*, an English-language newspaper devoted to the advancement of the Māori people. #7

IRIAKA MATIU RĀTANA OBE (1905-1981)

Born on the upper Whanganui River in 1905, Iriaka Rātana (Te Āti Haunui-a-Pāpārangi) lived at the Rātana Pā from the age of sixteen.

She won the Western Maori electorate for Labour in the November 1949 general election, succeeding her husband Matiu Ratana to become the first woman to represent Maori in the Aotearoa/New Zealand parliament. Pregnant at the time of the selection, she gave birth to her youngest daughter one month after she had been elected. She served in parliament for twenty years, working to improve the living standards and welfare of her people.

'She upheld the Treaty of Waitangi as a 'beacon light' for race relations. She was a member of the Maori Affairs Committee, of the Ngarimu VC and 28th (Maori) Battalion Memorial Scholarship Fund Board and of the Maori Purposes Fund Board, and was elected to the Aotea and Waikato–Maniapoto District Maori Land Boards.' #8

GROUP AT WEDDING OF NINIWA-I-TE-RANGI AND TAMAIHOTUA APORO IN THE WAIRARAPA, CA 1900. STANDING (LEFT TO RIGHT): HARE HONGI (H M STOWELL), MRS TOMIRI TE AWA, ALF NEEDHAM. SEATED (LEFT TO RIGHT): TAMAIHOTUA APORO, NINIWA-I-TE-RANGI.

Henry Smith Fish

Despite first being elected to Parliament in 1881, as well as serving 20 years on the Dunedin City Council — including six as mayor — and serving in several other civic roles, Fish is now remembered more for the reputation he gained as 'conceited, rude and untrustworthy. Rumours of dubious morality and petty corruption stuck to him, especially when it was discovered he falsified signatures on anti-suffrage petitions.

It was said female voting power eventually saw him lose both his mayoralty in 1892 and his re-election to Parliament in 1893. In an address Marion Hatton, the president of the Dunedin Women's Franchise League, in 1892, said:

'There is just one matter on which Mr Fish and the women of Dunedin are quite agreed (and only one), that is, when we women of Dunedin do get the franchise, there will be an end of Mr Fish, and he knows it!' (North Otago Times, 5 July 1892.)

THE ANTI-SUFFRAGE VIEW

Just who, exactly, fought against the moves to give women the vote? And why?

Because the call for suffrage was led by the WCTU, who opposed the sale of alcohol, those in the business of selling alcohol came out strongly to oppose the women's work. The liquor lobby distributed anti-suffrage petitions in their establishments in 1892. One of their supporters, Henry Fish of Dunedin, paid his anti-suffrage campaigners on the basis of how many signatures they obtained, resulting in

DO YOU THINK...

opinions such as this still exist today? What does it tell us about the general attitude towards women at the time?

5000 signatures. Later it was discovered, however, that some of names were made-up, some had been paid to sign, and still others were women who had been tricked into thinking they were signing to support suffrage.

It wasn't only the liquor lobby who were against the idea of women's suffrage. The notion that women could take a more equal place in society was hotly rejected by many men, who did not want the balance of their power shifted. Questions were asked such as whether the granting of voting rights to women would challenge a husband's 'manliness' and whether reform would lead to unthinkable role reversals where the wife worked and husbands wore the apron. [#9]

The Churches were divided on the issue, with the Catholic Church especially strong in its opposition. There was concern suffrage was a threat to family life and would lead to the destruction of 'traditional family values', with women abandoning their families and rejecting their feminine roles. Broader claims were made as well, such as that women were too emotional to take part in politics and that the finances and reputation of the colony would be negatively affected. Those women suffragists who were married were told to go home and focus on the well-being of their husbands and children; those unmarried or childless were described as 'old maids, or wives who are not mothers, or eccentrics.' [#10]

One parliamentary member, Mr. Wi Pere, claimed the distraction of having women in Parliament was greatly concerning. He said: *"Although I am getting up in years I must confess I should be affected by a weakness of that sort. If the honourable gentlemen in charge of the Bill would introduce a clause providing that only plain women should be allowed to come into the House, I think the source of danger would be removed, but if any beautiful ladies were sent to this House I am sure they would lead astray the tender hearts of some honourable gentlemen, particularly the elder members of the House. I say in conclusion that if attractive ladies are allowed into this House I am quite certain that my own wife will never consent to my returning here."* [#11]

ARE WE THERE YET?
Where are we at and what does it all mean?

With the granting of the vote to women, right from the first election it was clear that politicians would now have to more fully consider women's rights and concerns as they moved forwards. The ripples from this historic win spread right around the globe, an inspiration to other suffragists still fighting for voting rights in their own countries. Australia was quick to follow Aotearoa/New Zealand: South Australia gave women the vote in 1894, Western Australia in 1899, and the Australian Commonwealth government followed suit in 1902, except for Aboriginal women. It wasn't until 1962 that the Menzies Government amended the Commonwealth Electoral Act to give all indigenous people the right to enrol and vote in Commonwealth elections (irrespective of their voting rights at the state level.)

In Aotearoa/New Zealand, we saw the rise of several crucial women's organisations, such as the **National Council of Women** (with Kate Sheppard appointed as their first president), the **NZ Women's Institute**, the **Māori Women's Welfare League**, the **NZ Federation of University Women and the Business and**

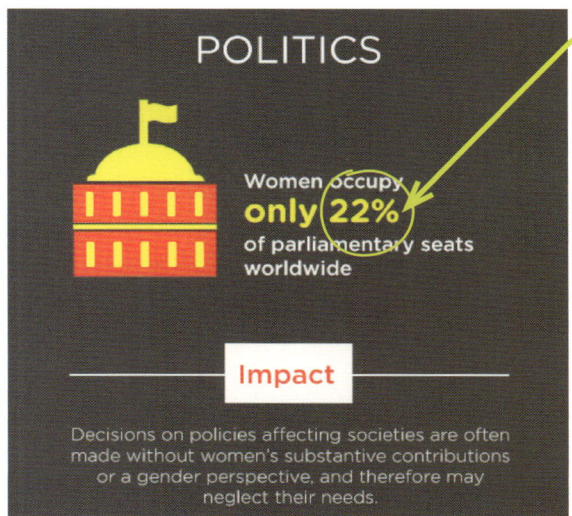

DETAIL FROM THE MANY FORMS OF DISCRIMINATION AS IT APPEARS ON THE UN WOMEN INFOGRAPHIC: HUMAN RIGHTS OF WOMEN, DATED DECEMBER 2015.

Professional Women's Clubs — all of which still continue in various forms today.

But, even with this growing acceptance of women's rights, Aotearoa/New Zealand women still weren't allowed to stand for Parliament until 1919. The first female Member of Parliament (Elizabeth McCombs) wasn't elected until 1933 – 40 years after the historic suffrage win. Indeed, the number of female MPs did not even reach double figures until the mid-1980s. It wasn't until the switch to the MMP (Mixed Member Proportional) voting system in 1996 that we started to see a significant rise in the numbers of women representing us, with 35 women elected (almost 30% of the Parliament.) Since then there has been small but steady growth, with the 2017 general election seeing a mix of 38% women to 62% men.

It took until 1947 for Aotearoa/New Zealand women to see Mabel Howard named as the first female Cabinet Minister, 1949 for Iriaka Ratana to become the first female Māori MP, 1972 for Whetu Tirikatene-Sullivan to become the first female Māori Cabinet Minister, and 1997 for Jenny Shipley to become our first female Prime Minister after replacing Jim Bolger as leader of the National Party. Our first elected female Prime Minister was Helen Clark in 1999. She would continue in this position for nine years, making her Aotearoa/New Zealand's 5th-longest-serving PM. In 2017, Jacinda Ardern became our 40th (and second elected female) Prime Minister, breaking new records by becoming the world's youngest female head of government at age 37. She is also the first NZ Prime Minister to bear a child while in office.

NUMBER OF MPS IN PARLIMENT

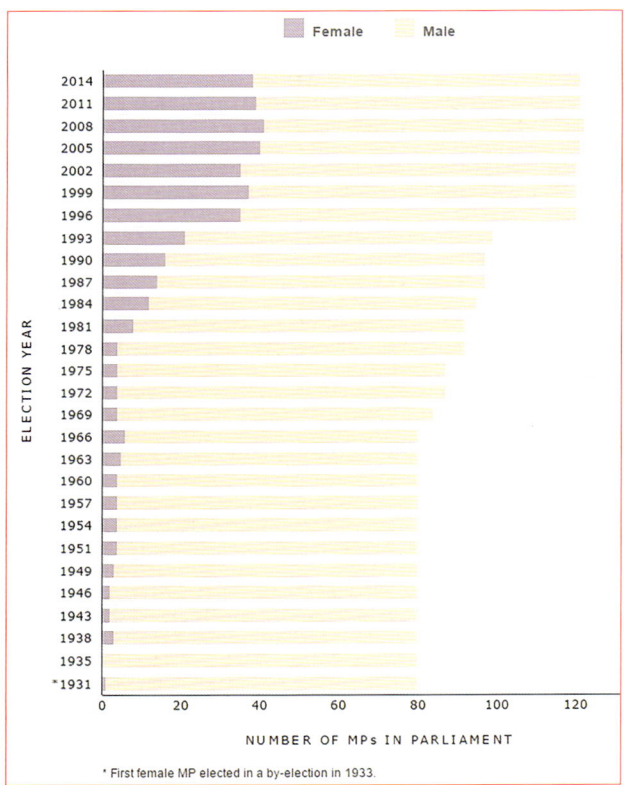

THE 2017 GENERAL ELECTION SAW 46 WOMEN ELECTED TO PARLIAMENT.

WHAT DOES ALL THIS MEAN TO EVERYDAY AOTEAROA/NEW ZEALAND WOMEN'S LIVES TODAY?

Without women's voices raising the very real issues both women and their children have to face, many of the protections in place for the vulnerable, and for victims, may not have found their way into law. For instance:

- **1898: A new Divorce Act** was passed after women began demanding equality in family matters. Until 1867 anyone wishing to divorce had to apply to the English courts. In 1867 Aotearoa/New Zealand's first divorce law, the **Divorce and Matrimonial Causes Act**, was passed, allowing either husband or wife to seek a divorce. But while a man only needed to prove adultery on the part of his wife to gain a divorce, a wife had to prove her husband had committed adultery *plus* sodomy, incest, bestiality, bigamy, rape or extreme cruelty. With the passing of the Divorce Act in 1898, adultery alone became enough for either men or women to be divorced. New grounds included: five years' desertion; refusal to cohabit when ordered to by the Court; drunkenness and failure to support the family (husband) or drunkenness and neglect of domestic duties (wife); or seven or more years' imprisonment for the attempted murder of one's spouse.[#12]

- **1904: The Midwives Registration Act** was passed, creating new job opportunities for women and ensuring better outcomes for mothers and babies.

- **1919: Women's Parliamentary Rights Act** was passed, putting women on the same footing as men in their ability to run for parliament.

- **1925: The Child Welfare Act**, the 1926 **Family Allowances Act** and the 1938 **Social Security Act** were all designed to benefit vulnerable families and individuals, and provide financial support.

- **Various Acts covering sexual assault crimes**, including non-consent, statutory rape, marital rape, and domestic violence protections, were designed to provide better safeguards and more supportive treatment of victims, as well as appropriate punishments for offenders. [10]
- **1972: The Equal Pay Act** was another step in the advancement of women politically and economically.
- **1976: The Domicile Act** provided women with more freedom, enabling them to be free from the control of their husbands.
- **1977: The Human Rights Commissions Act** was yet another act advancing the status of women and encouraging equality between different genders.
- **1990: The Employment Equality Act** was another law aimed at bridging the gap between male and female pay-rates.

This ongoing commitment to supporting women and children, and raising their status and freedoms to equal those of men, may have begun with the hard work of the suffragists, but it is still a work in progress. Thanks to them, the idea that women can only occupy domestic roles is now largely a thing of the past in Aotearoa/New Zealand society, and we are able to see women taking an ever more active role in shaping the political and social landscape of the country. Imagine how Kate Sheppard would have felt if she'd known that one day we'd see a woman chosen as Prime Minister, Governor General, Speaker of the House of Representatives, Attorney General and Chief Justice?

But does this mean the fight is over? Sadly no. Pay equality and paid parental leave are still works in progress, as is the goal of seeing women fill top seats in the corporate and business worlds. Issues around the reporting and conviction rates for sexual abuse/assaults and domestic violence are still ongoing. When Jacinda Ardern was elected as Prime Minister, she still had to face personal questions about whether she'd have children and if this would prevent her doing a good job, despite no male leader ever having been asked such questions. And how women and girls are depicted in the media still works to underline the sexist attitudes of the past.

In a discussion between current Prime Minister Jacinda Ardern and past Prime Minister Helen Clark, as part of the 125-year anniversary of suffrage in 2018, Clark was asked what was the next significant barrier for Aotearoa/New Zealand women to overcome?

> Helen Clark replied:
> 'I look at the issue of sexual and gender-based violence and I say if a woman cannot be safe in her home, if she cannot be safe in her community, this is an incredible blight on her developing her full potential. You'll never have gender equity while these rates of violence persist. It's the biggest problem in New Zealand.' [13]

Other high-profile women, interviewed for the NZ Herald's Suffrage issue (Sept 15, 2018), also spoke of their hopes and concerns for women, and their thoughts about the early suffragists.

Dr Kiri Dell (Ngāti Porou):
'The suffrage movement started to give women a voice in the power structures that shape and influence our lives. But a vast section of women in Māori society still have no voice. Socio-economic deprivation, tied to the legacy of colonisation and the persistence of un/conscious sexual and racial biases, disempowers us as both citizens and people. . . '

Professor Jane Godfrey:
'If I could wave a magic wand, I'd have an equal distribution of women and men in business at all levels, based on merit. That's what we are working towards but it won't happen overnight.'

Dr Margaret Dudley:
'The suffragettes showed all of us that women can be leaders in any field they choose.'

Associate Professor Elana Taipapaki Curtis:
'We think we've reached a place where males and females are on the same playing field but it's not true. While we think that, we'll never fix the problem.'

Emeritus Professor Raewyn Dalziel:
'We should not underestimate the strength of the challenge that the women's vote posed to the status quo and the boldness of this particular "leap in the dark".'

WOULD YOU BE PREPARED, AS THE SUFFRAGISTS WERE, TO TAKE UP THE FIGHT? AS KATE SHEPPARD SAID:

"The question for me is whether we can keep Earth a safe, pleasant place for humankind and the ecosystems we rely on…Do not think your single vote does not matter much. The rain that refreshes the parched ground is made up of single drops."

The suffrage movement teaches us that if women stand together and fight for the rights they deserve, progress can be made towards a fairer and more equitable world for all.

WANT TO FIND OUT MORE?
BOOKS:
- Neill Atkinson, *Adventures in democracy: a history of the vote in New Zealand,* University of Otago Press, Dunedin, 2003
- Sandra Coney, *Standing in the sunshine: a history of New Zealand women since they won the vote*, Viking, Auckland, 1993
- Caroline Daley and Melanie Nolan (eds), *Suffrage and beyond: international feminist perspectives*, Auckland University Press, Auckland, 1994
- Judith Devaliant, *Kate Sheppard: a biography*, Penguin Books, Auckland, 1992
- Patricia Grimshaw, *Women's suffrage in New Zealand,* 2nd edn, University of Auckland Press, Auckland, 1987
- Margaret Lovell-Smith (ed.), *The woman question: writings by the women who won the vote*, New Women's Press, Auckland, 1992

- Tania Rei, *Māori Women and the Vote*. Wellington: Huia Publishers, 1993.
- Janet McCallum, *Women in the House: Members of Parliament in New Zealand*, Cape Catley, Picton, 1993
- *The suffragists: women who worked for the vote. Essays from the Dictionary of New Zealand biography*, Bridget Williams Books/Department of Internal Affairs, Wellington, 1993.
- Bronwyn Labrum (ed.) *Women Now: The Legacy of Female Suffrage*, Te Papa Press, 2018
- Maria Gill and Marco Ivancic, *Kate Sheppard: Leading the Way for Women,* Scholastic, 2018
- Barbara Brookes, *A History of New Zealand Women*, Bridget Williams Books, 2018.
- Jenny Coleman, *Polly Plum: A Firm and Earnest Women's Advocate,* Mary Ann Colclough 1836-1885, Otago University Press, 2017.

WEBSITES:

- The essay *Pao Pao Pao*, by Tina Makereti (which you can read at: https://www.radionz.co.nz/programmes/news-extras/story/2018663006/pao-pao-pao-essay-chapter-by-tina-makereti-from-book-women-now-the-legacy-of-female-suffrage)
- http://www.nzedge.com/legends/kate-sheppard
- https://tear.govt.nz/en/biographies
- The NZ History website from the Ministry for Culture and Heritage. https://nzhistory.govt.nz/
- http://nzetc.victoria.ac.nz/tm/scholarly/name-457099.html
- Universal Franchise In New Zealand https://simranwomenssuffrage.weebly.com/

THESE LETTERS TO AND FROM 'POLLY PLUM' (MARY ANN COLCLOUGH) APPEARED IN THE *NEW ZEALAND HERALD* ON 16 AND 18 AUGUST 1871.

QUESTIONS FOR POLLY PLUM BY JELLABY PATER (1871)

QUESTIONS FOR POLLY PLUM.
To the Editor of the Herald.

SIR,—I would like, through the medium of your columns, to ask " Polly Plum" to state in a few short petty sentences, without any of that circumlocution which characterises her letters, what she demands as " Women's Rights"? I have read the whole of the controversy (?) between her and her various correspondents, but as yet fail to see what she aims at. Her letters to me are "full of sound and fury", but after reading them through they "signify nothing". After patiently reading everything emanating from her during the past six months, I am still in a state of blissful ignorance as to the nature of the so-called 'rights' she claims for women. Her ideas are so wrapt up in a cloud of words that it is impossible to sift the grain of wheat (if there is one) from the bagful of chaff in which her letters are smothered. — Please answer the following questions seriatim: — 1st. What rights are they which "P. P." desires for women? 2nd. Has not woman a perfectly legal right under the present law to protect her own property and secure it to herself by means of a marriage settlement? 3rd. On what does she ground her idea that women generally are dissatisfied with their present position? 4th. Setting aside the present agitators — Mill, Miss Nightingale, and others — that 'P. P.' is so fond of quoting, can she state on her veracity that she knows six married ladies in Auckland who are dissatisfied with their present legal position? 5th. Can 'P. P.' bring to bear any text of Scripture which is violated by the present legal position of women? In conclusion, I would again ask 'Polly Plum' to reply in terse sentences to these questions, to avoid circumlocution, far-fetched similes, and recondite allusions. — I am, &c,

JELLABY PATER.

ANSWERS TO 'JELLABY PATER' BY POLLY PLUM (1871)

SIR, – The enclosed are answers for 'Jellaby Pater', with 'Polly Plum's' compliments, hoping to see the day when he shall be added to the list of those who, while upholding Christianity, hate oppression.
– I am, &c, POLLY PLUM
Wednesday, August 16, 1871.

1st. The right, as thinking, reasoning beings, to decide for themselves what is best for their own happiness. If they were satisfied with man's decision, this agitation for change would not be.

2nd. A woman can only protect property she has before marriage. Men, unless proved bad and incapable, can claim all property and earnings after marriage. This the writer has experienced, her husband – not a bad, but a thoroughly unbusiness-like, unenergetic man – spent pounds and pounds of his wife's earnings in profitless, and even in ruinous speculations, and on one occasion all the little home comforts she had gathered around her, by unremitting toil, were seized through some of his mistakes, and she and two little children, the eldest not two years old, were left on the bare floor.

3rd. The immense movement in favour of a change answers that question.

4th. On my veracity, 75 per cent of my married lady friends are opposed to the present law, many of them happy enough themselves but knowing of wrongs, evils, and injustice that make them in favour of 'woman's rights'. My experience in Auckland – for I have had no experience in these matters elsewhere – goes to prove that young single ladies are those who are most opposed to the new view, their ideas of marriage being simply ideal, and that married ladies are not always sincere with their husbands in this matter. It is not to their interests to be so. They offend their husband, make domestic broils, and can at present gain nothing, and lose much comfort. Thackeray, in Denis Duval, says, 'But you don't expect sincerity and subservience'.

5th. Christ's rule of life, 'Do unto others as ye would they should do unto you', and the whole spirit of Gospel doctrine, is opposed to arbitrarily deciding for anybody what is best for them.

[We think it but fair to publish our fair correspondent's reply. The correspondence is now closed. – Ed. N.Z.H.]

THE GREAT DIVIDE

1981 SPRINGBOK TOUR

" A Springbok Tour would engender the greatest eruption of violence this country has ever known…more important however is the effect which a decision to proceed with the tour would have in tarnishing New Zealand's image as a multicultural community"
Norman Kirk (29th Prime Minister of Aotearoa/New Zealand from 1972 until his sudden death in 1974)[14]

"A National Government would welcome a Springbok team to New Zealand even if there were threats of violence and civil strife… I believe sporting contracts will be one of six major issues of the election campaign…this is one issue on which people will change their vote" Robert Muldoon (31st Prime Minister of Aotearoa/New Zealand from 1975 to 1984) [14]

"If the Government unleashes the tiger and then cries wolf there will be a backlash."
David Lange, (32nd Prime Minister of Aotearoa/New Zealand from 1984 to 1989) [15]

For many Aotearoa/New Zealanders old enough to have lived through the turmoil of the 1981 Springbok Rugby Tour, it stands as a defining moment that shifted us from seeing ourselves as loyal subjects of a 'Britain of the South' [16] to citizens of an independent Pacific nation, Aotearoa/New Zealand, whose unified voice could influence the world beyond our shores. For others it's seen as the moment Aotearoa/New Zealand lost its innocence as a country. For most, such was the depth of feeling, it can still prompt reactions that range from anger to pride to shame.

A LONE PROTESTER IS WATCHED BY THE POLICE LINE DURING PROTESTS, 15 AUGUST 1981.

No matter where people stand, it's true to say that the protests which greeted the Springboks, South Africa's national rugby team, the Springboks, in 1981, sparked off one of the most violent and controversial series of events in Aotearoa/New Zealand's history. For 56 days between July and September of that year, New Zealanders fought against each other in the biggest civil uprising since the 1951 waterfront dispute *(To find out more about the Waterfront Dispute refer to* https://nzhistory.govt.nz/politics/the-1951-waterfront-dispute*)*. More than 150,000 people took part in over 200 demonstrations in 28 towns and cities. Around 1,500 people were charged with offences that arose from the protests and the police spent an estimated $15 million on 'Operation Rugby' to defend the tour.[16]

At its heart, the divide was between those who believed that we should refuse to engage with South Africa until it changed its racist laws, and those who thought politics had no place in sport and that direct engagement would be a better pathway towards change, leading by example.

To understand how this all came to pass, first we need to dig into the situation in South Africa at the time. What was it about this distant country that enraged so many people? And why did the anti-tour protesters believe their actions could make change for good?

APARTHEID

The word '**apartheid**' literally means 'separateness', 'apart-hood' or 'the state of being apart', but in a bigger sense it stands for the repressive and racist system of government that existed in South Africa between 1948 and 1994.

This system was based on the idea of **white supremacy** and control of the 'black' majority of the population (classified as either African/Bantu, Coloured, Asian or Indian) in such a way that it only benefitted (politically and economically) the **minority Afrikaners** and other 'whites' who lived there.

Under apartheid, all 'non-white' South Africans were forced to live in separate areas, use different public facilities (such as schools, hospitals, public toilets, shops, and transport) and were banned from mixing with 'white' South Africans unless employed by them (and, even then, they were kept separate.) Inter-racial relationships or marriages were treated as a crime, and 'non-whites' were not allowed to vote or choose where to live, and had to carry passes to move outside restricted areas. People were classified by the colour of their skin or ancestry, splitting families in instances where parents were classified as 'white' and their children as 'coloured', 'African'/'Bantu' or 'Asian' (or the other way around).

From 1960 to 1983, 3.5 million 'non-white' South Africans were forced from their homes and shifted into **segregated** neighbourhoods, where they were driven into poverty and hopelessness, in one of the biggest mass removals in modern history ("South Africa – Overcoming Apartheid". African Studies Center of Michigan State University). Nearly every right you currently enjoy as a citizen of a democratic country was denied them, and this racist attitude was written into laws and brutally policed.

HOW ON EARTH DID THIS COME ABOUT?

From the timeline on Pgs 36-39 we can see how these racist measures were built on over time,

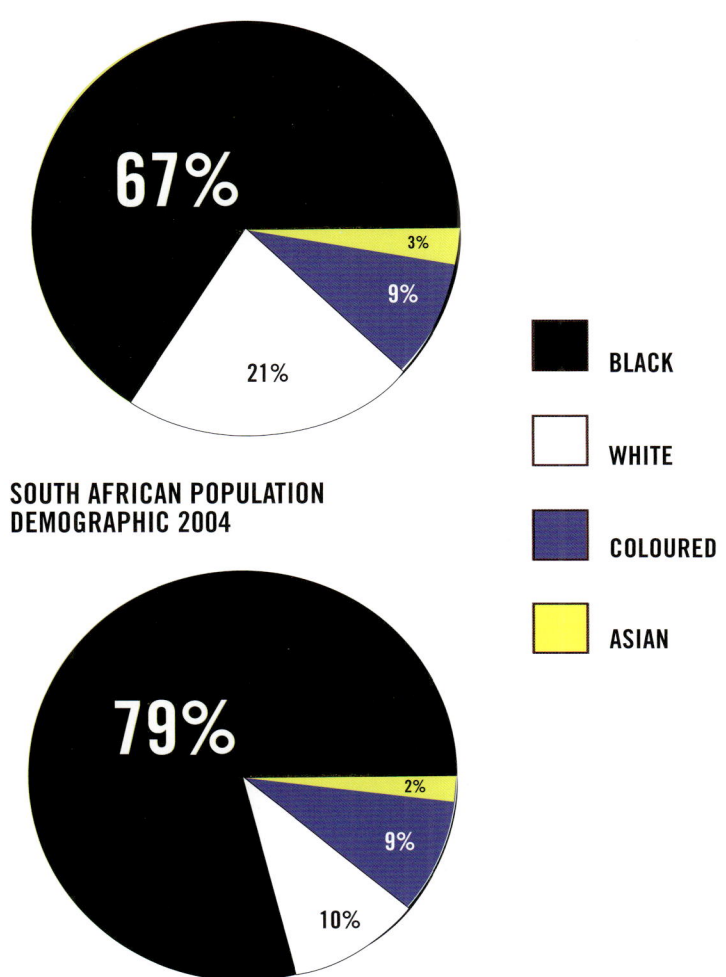

SOUTH AFRICAN POPULATION DEMOGRAPHIC 1911 #18

- 67% BLACK
- 21% WHITE
- 9% COLOURED
- 3% ASIAN

SOUTH AFRICAN POPULATION DEMOGRAPHIC 2004

- 79% BLACK
- 10% WHITE
- 9% COLOURED
- 2% ASIAN

NB: THE 2011 CENSUS FIGURES FOR THESE GROUPS WERE BLACK AFRICAN AT 80.2%, WHITE AT 8.4%, COLOURED AT 8.8%, INDIAN/ASIAN AT 2.5%, AND OTHER/UNSPECIFIED AT 0.5% #19

DURBAN SIGN THAT STATES THE BEACH IS FOR WHITES ONLY UNDER SECTION 37 OF THE DURBAN BEACH BY-LAWS. THE LANGUAGES ARE ENGLISH, AFRIKAANS AND ZULU – THE LANGUAGE OF THE BLACK POPULATION GROUP IN THE DURBAN AREA

"If the principle of permanent residence for the black man in the area of the white is accepted then it is the beginning of the end of civilisation as we know it in this country."
(Pieter W. Botha, leader of South Africa from 1978 to 1989.) #17

KEY WORD & PHRASES

Afrikaner: an Afrikaans-speaking 'white' person in South Africa, especially one descended from the Dutch and Huguenot settlers of the 17th century.

Apartheid: a policy that legalised racial segregation and political and economic discrimination against non-'whites'.

Boycott: to withdraw from commercial or social relations with a country, organization, or person as a punishment or protest.

Colonised/colonisation: the action or process of settling among and establishing control over the indigenous people of an area.

Homelands: or Bantustans, were areas established by the Apartheid Government to move the majority of the 'black' population out of the urban areas of South Africa. These 'homelands' were given the responsibility of running their own independent governments, thus denying them protection and any remaining rights a 'black' could have in South Africa.

Indentured labourer: an employee (indenturee) within a system of unfree labour who is bound by a signed or forced contract (indenture) to work for a particular employer for a fixed time. The contract often lets the employer sell the labour of an indenturee to a third party.

Minority: the smaller number or part, especially a number or part representing less than half of the whole.

Mobilise: organise and encourage (a group of people) to take collective action in pursuit of a particular objective.

Nationalist: a person with strong patriotic feelings, especially one who believes in the superiority of their country over others.

Pass Laws: A form of internal passport system designed to segregate the population, manage growth of towns and cities, and control migrant labour. Also known as the **Natives Law**, pass laws severely limited the movements of not only 'black' African citizens, but other peoples as well, requiring them to carry pass books when outside their homelands or designated areas. Pass laws would be one of the dominant features of the country's apartheid system, until it was effectively ended in 1986.

Repression: the action of subduing someone or something by force.

Segregate: set apart from the rest or from each other; isolate or divide.

Totalitarian: a form of rule in which the government attempts to maintain control over a society, including all aspects of the public and private lives of its citizens. Rule by terror.

White Supremacy: the belief that 'white' people are superior to those of all other races, especially the 'black' race, and should therefore dominate society.

steadily chipping away at human rights, from as far back as the eighteenth century. Keep in mind that the indigenous people of Southern Africa had already been **colonised** by both the Dutch and British, setting the scene for what was to come. Why is it important to document these measures? They reflect the same steady erosion of rights as seen in other **totalitarian** regimes, from the Nazis' rise in Germany to Stalin's Soviet Russia, Mussolini's Italy, Mao Zedong's People's Republic of China and North Korea. By recognising the patterns we can watch for signs of democratic and human rights 'slipPg' within our own societies.

SIGNS OF SEGREGATION.

SHOP SIGN: NON-WHITE SHOP THIS NOTICE IS DISPLAYED IN ACCORDANCE WITH THE PROVISIONS OF THE SHOP HOURS ORDINANCE. 1959.

"Black people were separated according to the language they speak, age, level of education and level of importance to the Apartheid regime. Black people were taught Bantu Education, a syllabus that trained blacks how to be of better service to their slave Baas (Afrikaner for 'white master'). Therefore, the young and able-bodied were moved to shanty towns next to mines, women worked as domestic workers, the less educated worked in farms and lived with their Baas, and the old and fragile were moved to Transkei." [20]

Aviwe AV Ndyaluvane

HOW WOULD YOU FEEL?

As you read this, imagine if you were alive at the time and were considered 'non-white'. How must it have felt to see your human rights so quickly and ruthlessly stolen away? How must it have felt to be told you were a foreigner in your own country and forcibly wrenched from your home? Or talked about solely in terms of your skin colour? For indigenous people everywhere who have been colonised this is a reality. Only by truly exploring the core issues can we understand why the battle waged by anti-Springbok Tour protesters was so fiercely fought.

SOUTH AFRICA'S SLIPPERY SLIDE INTO AN APARTHEID STATE #21

For more than a century, laws were passed or rewritten by the minority rulers to increase their powers and to diminish the rights and freedoms of the non-white population.

1797: All Khoikhoi (a group of Khoisan people native to southwestern Africa) are required to carry 'passes' if moving around the country for any purpose.

1806: The Cape Articles of Capitulation separated South African law from English Common Law and allowed South Africa to act independently of the British Empire in terms of setting laws.

1835: After the United Kingdom's Abolition Act of 1833, abolishing slavery throughout the British Empire, Ordinance 1 was passed to change the status of slaves to indentured labourers (in reality still slavery, just with a different title.)

1848: Ordinance 3 introduced an indenture system for Xhosa people (a Bantu ethnic group of Southern Africa), again little different from slavery. This was followed by various pieces of legislation designed to further limit freedom of unskilled and indentured workers, and to stop mixing between the races.

1894: The Franchise and Ballot Act put limits on 'black' voters, based on finances and education. That same year, the Natal Legislative Assembly Bill was passed into law, despite being opposed by **Mahatma Gandhi** of **India**, who submitted a petition signed by 10,000 Indians to the **Natal** Government. It deprived those of Indian origin the right to vote, while that same year the Glen Grey Act limited the amount of land 'non-white' Africans were allowed to own.

1905: The General Pass Regulations Act denied all 'blacks' the vote and limited them to fixed areas. It also put in the place the infamous pass system (see key words).

1906: All Indians were required to register and carry passes. (Many Indians in South Africa are descendants of migrants from colonial India (South Asia) during late 19th-century through early 20th-century.)

1910: The Union of South Africa was created as a self-governing dominion (semi-independent territories under the wing of the British Crown.) The South Africa Act gave all whites the vote, handing them complete political control over all other racial groups while removing the right of 'blacks' to sit in Parliament.

1913: The Native Land Act was designed to force 'blacks' into specified locations.

1923: the Urban Areas Act introduced residential (housing) segregation and provided cheap labour for industries controlled by 'whites'.

1926: The Colour Bar Act prevented 'black' mine workers from practising skilled trades.

ABOVE: SEGREGATION SIGNAGE

TOP: CHILDREN SIT ON A BENCH AT THE WATERFRONT IN DURBAN, SOUTH AFRICA, MAY 27, 1960.

RIGHT: PEOPLE WATCHING A SPORTS GAME IN APARTHEID SOUTH AFRICA.

TIMELINE

1927: The Native Administration Act made the British Crown the supreme ruler over all African affairs, rather than traditional paramount chiefs.

1936: The Native Land and Trust Act extended the Native Land Act, and the Representation of Natives Act removed the last 'black' voters from the Cape roll and instead elected another three 'whites' to Parliament.

1946: The Asiatic Land Tenure Bill banned land sales to Indians.

1948: In the lead-up to the 1948 election, Afrikaner nationalists offered voters a new policy to ensure continued 'white' domination. The policy, from a theory drafted by Hendrick Verwoerd (who would later serve as prime minister from 1958 until his assassination in 1966), asserted that segregation should be extended to every part of South African law and life. His National Party called the new policy 'Apartheid' and this catapulted them into government with an eight-vote parliamentary lead.

1949: The Prohibition of Mixed Marriages Act banned marriages between different races.

1950: The Population Registration Act formalised radical classification and introduced an identity card for all people over 18 years of age which specified their racial group. Official boards were set up to decide on people's race if it was unclear, prompting many families to be split when family members were assigned to different races. Also in 1950, the Group Areas Act imposed separate areas to live for separate races, and the Immorality Act made sexual relations between people of different races a crime. The Suppression of Communism Act was also introduced, banning any party who supported Communism (though, in reality, this Act was used to swoop on anyone who opposed government policy.) 'Disorderly' gatherings were also banned as a move to stifle resistance.

1951: The Prevention of Illegal Squatting Act allowed the government to demolish 'black' shanty towns (slums) and forced 'white' employers to build housing for any 'black' workers allowed to live in cities reserved for 'whites'. The Bantu Authorities Act was also passed, creating separate government structures for 'blacks' and 'whites' – the first part of a plan to shift people into 'homelands'.

1952: The High Court of Parliament Bill was introduced, giving Parliament the power to overturn court decisions. With this, any remaining democratic rights in South Africa could be 'legally' overruled.

1953: The Reservation of Separate Amenities Act reserved certain public areas for particular races, including beaches, buses, trains, hospitals, cinemas, shops, schools and universities and even park benches. More and more signs started appearing declaring 'whites only.' The Bantu Education Act brought about a separate system of education for 'black' South Africans, designed to prepare them for lives as labourers.

1956 – A new law allowed 'coloureds' the right to elect four representatives to Parliament. This was overturned again in 1969. Until this point, women (for the most part) had been exempt from 'pass' laws; this now changed.

A POSTER MADE BY THE ANTI-APARTHEID MOVEMENT IN THE UNITED KINGDOM HIGHLIGHTS THE SEGREGATION RULES

1958: The policy of 'separate development' came in being, with a goal to making each of the 'homelands' independent. The government justified this by saying: "(the) policy is not a policy of discrimination on the grounds of race or colour, but a policy of differentiation on the ground of nationhood, of different nations, granting to each self-determination within the borders of their homelands – hence this policy of separate development." In other words, now 'blacks' would no longer be thought of as citizens of South Africa, instead becoming citizens of the independent 'homelands' system who could only work in South Africa as foreign migrant labourers on temporary work permits. Many 'black' South Africans were forcibly removed from cities and banished to their appointed 'homelands.' Ten 'homelands' were established for different ethnic groups and their people issued passports instead of passes.

1959: The Promotion of Black Self-Government Act reinforced the 'homelands' approach and set them up for self-government. Separate universities were created for 'black', 'coloured' and Indian people and existing universities were not allowed to enrol new 'black' students. Economic as well as political separation entrenched poverty in the 'homelands' (see Incomes graph on Pg 40).

RIGHT: APARTHEID SIGN IN ENGLISH AND AFRIKANS

ABOVE: ROAD SIGN, 1956, HULTON ARCHIVE

1961: South Africa becomes a republic in a narrowly won referendum of 'white' voters. A decision is made to continue with apartheid.

1967: Legislation is put in place to shift industrial production from 'white' cities to the 'homelands'. During the 1960s, 1970s and early 1980s government-imposed 'resettlement' forced millions of people to relocate. One of the most publicised took place in the 1950s, when 60,000 people were moved from Johannesburg to the new township of Soweto. Many forced removals happened in the early hours of morning, when people were loaded onto trucks and moved elsewhere. #22

41

OTHER REPRESSION OF OPPORTUNITIES AND PROTECTIONS:

- Sports club membership was based on race. This is of particular significance to any discussion about the 1981 Springbok Tour.
- 'Blacks' were not allowed to run businesses or professional practices in 'white' designated areas.
- Trade unions were racially segregated, reducing their power.
- In the 1970s, the state spent ten times more on education for 'white' children (the minority).
- 'Blacks' were banned from buying hard liquor and could only buy inferior state-produced beer or brew their own liquor.
- 'Whites' owned almost all the industrial and agricultural land and the best residential land.
- 'Blacks' earning 360 rand (South African currency) for more a year had to pay taxes, while for 'whites' the tax threshold was 750 rand per year.

ANTI-APARTHEID GRAFFITI.

WHERE WAS THE LOCAL OPPOSITION?

'Nelson Mandela can rot in prison until he dies or I die, whichever takes longer.' P. W. Botha (leader of South Africa from 1978 to 1989)[#23]

Over the years, resistance within South Africa to apartheid took many forms, from non-violent protests and strikes, to political pressure and armed conflict. The government, in turn, responded with brutal police crackdowns, pushing many protesters even further down the road towards violent confrontation. This resistance sprang up in many different parts of society, 'whites' included, and several organisations emerged to fight for change.

Of these, the *African National Congress* (ANC) was to become the dominant force. In 1949, the ANC's youth wing took control of the organisation and started calling for a radical strategy to fight for 'black' rights. They believed that only mass campaigns could overthrow 'white' authority. Among those building the youth wing were activists **Oliver Tambo** and **Nelson Mandela.**

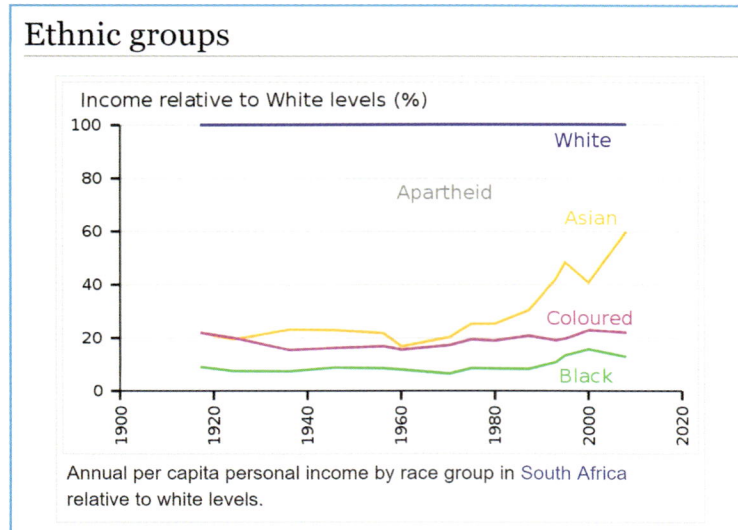

ANNUAL PER CAPITA PERSONAL INCOME BY RACE GROUP IN SOUTH AFRICA RELATIVE TO WHITE LEVELS

It was another organisation, however, that prompted one of the first chillingly brutal police actions. The *Pan Africanist Congress* (the PAC), formed from people dissatisfied with the ANC, organised a series of demonstrations against pass books in 1960. On March 21, 5,000 'black' protestors gathered outside of the Sharpeville township police station to voice their anger against pass laws. The police opened fire on the protestors, wounding more than 180 people and killing 69 others (including 8 women and 10 children), many of them shot in the back as they tried to escape. This event came to be known as the **Sharpeville Massacre**.

Consequently the government declared a State of Emergency, a measure that allowed them to override any laws that stood in their way. They ordered the arrest of more than 18,000 people, including leaders of the ANC and PAC, and banned both organisations. This drove the resistance underground, where some committed acts of sabotage and terrorism, while others fled overseas seeking safety and freedom.

By 1961, most of the protest leaders had been captured and executed or sentenced to lengthy prison terms. Despite these risks, others took up the call and organised mass demonstrations and strikes in the lead-up to South Africa being declared a republic. In response, the government gave police powers to arrest and detain people for up to twelve days (to keep them from 'spoiling' the celebrations). Many of the strike leaders were arrested and the police again brutally attacked the protesters.

Nelson Mandela, then aged 42, was one of the main protest organisers, and eventually called off the strike to prevent further police violence. But frustration at lack of progress saw the ANC then launch a military wing called *Umkhonto we Sizwe*, undertaking acts of sabotage on important state assets. Mandela, one of the founders of *Umkhonto we Sizwe,* was caught and jailed from 1963 until 1990. His imprisonment was to fuel the fire of overseas resistance to apartheid and the quest for his freedom was to become a powerful symbol in the fight for justice and freedom.

POLICE FIRED ON PROTESTORS ASSEMBLED OUTSIDE THE SHARPEVILLE POLICE STATION, 21 MARCH 1960. 69 WERE KILLED, MANY OF WHOME WERE SHOT IN THE BACK WHILE TRYING TO FLEE.

STUDENTS PROTESTING THE ENFORCEMENT OF AFRIKAN TEACHING IN SOWETO SCHOOLS WERE MEET WITH ARMED POLICE. BETWEEN 176-700 ARE THOUGHT TO HAVE BEEN KILLED.

The 1970s saw university students pick up on the ideas of the *Black Power* movement in the United States of America to form the *Black Consciousness Movement* (BC). This movement championed 'black pride' and celebrated African customs, rebuilding feelings of self-esteem eroded by the apartheid system. Again the government stepped in, and the BC's leader, **Steve Biko**, was taken into custody on the 18th August 1977, where he was beaten to death.

The date of Biko's murder and his name were to prove significant during the 1981 anti-Springbok Tour protests here in Aotearoa/New Zealand.

1976 saw secondary students in the township of Soweto rise up in protest after being forced to use the Afrikaans language (derived from the form of Dutch brought to the Cape by Protestant settlers in the 17th century) for their instruction. On June 16, the peaceful protest ended with police opening fire. Official reports said 23 students were killed, but the number of dead is more often given as 176, with estimates of up to 700. Pulitzer Prize-winning journalist Les Payne claimed that at least 850 murders were documented.[24] Despite this risk and slaughter, these courageous student organisations grew and were responsible for four school boycotts from 1980 to 1986.

Labour unions and churches also braved the wrath of the government and undertook protests and overseas lobbying to halt apartheid. Archbishop **Desmond Tutu** became an outspoken critic both at home and internationally and, over time, up to twenty percent of the 'white' population joined the opposition to the apartheid system.

A BLACK SASH PROTEST.

THE BLACK SASH

Founded in 1955, the Black Sash organisation was a group of white women who protested the abolishment of black voting rights. Participants would stand quietly in public locations wearing a symbolic black sash. They also set up legal advice centres to assist Africans with governmental issues. These advice centres continue to operate today, providing paralegal services and conducting human rights monitoring, education and research.

WHAT ABOUT OVERSEAS SUPPORT FOR THE ANTI-APARTHEID MOVEMENT?

We stand here today to salute the United Nations Organization and its member states, both singly and collectively, for joining forces with the masses of our people in a common struggle that has brought about our emancipation and pushed back the frontiers of racism. Nelson Mandela, to the United Nations as South African President in 1994.[25]

From 1946, the United Nations had South Africa in their sights, but it wasn't until the 1960 Sharpeville Massacre that the Security Council took concerted action — demanding an end to the segregation and discrimination. Over the following years, several resolutions condemned apartheid, and in 1966 the U.N. General Assembly announced that 21 of March would thereafter be known as the *International Day for the Elimination of Racial Discrimination*, in memory of the Sharpeville Massacre.

A motion to expel South Africa from the UN in 1974 was won, but then vetoed by the UK, US and France, all major trading partners with the country. Weapon embargoes (bans) and other trade sanctions were imposed over the years, along with cultural boycotts and sporting boycotts, which began in the mid-1950s. It was the call for sporting boycotts that would fire up the protest movement here in Aotearoa/New Zealand in 1981.

WHY SHOULD WE CARE?

For a country and *all* its citizens to thrive, the bottom line for any system of government is the protection of individual human rights. The UN's *Universal Declaration of Human Rights* states that:

. . . the recognition of the inherent dignity and of the equal and inalienable rights of all members of the human family is the foundation of freedom, justice and peace in the world and that disregard and contempt for human rights have resulted in barbarous acts which have outraged the conscience of mankind, and the advent of a world in which human beings shall enjoy freedom of speech and belief and freedom from fear and want has been proclaimed as the highest aspiration of the common people.[26]

This emphasises that part of being a good global citizen is not only caring about these rights in our own country, but ensuring that others are able to enjoy the same protective rights in their own countries. Without these human rights we have no economic rights and are consigned to perpetual poverty.

CUT TO AOTEAROA/NEW ZEALAND . . .

The protests against the 1981 Springbok Tour did not just spring out of nowhere. As a nation who thought of rugby as our national sport, the rivalry between the All Blacks and the Springboks was legendary, with many Aotearoa/New Zealand players considering their games against the Springboks the pinnacle of their careers.

The first official series between the two countries took place here in 1921, well before the worst of the apartheid years. But, even then, the South African practice of segregating sport was causing comment. After a win over the NZ Māori XV team in Napier, one South African journalist reported back in a cable his shock at 'white' spectators cheering on the Māori team:

Bad enough having to play officially designated New Zealand Natives, but [the] spectacle [of] thousands [of] Europeans frantically cheering on [a] band of coloured men to defeat members of [their] own race was too much for [the] Springboks[,] who frankly [were] disgusted.[27]

On their next tour to Aotearoa/New Zealand in 1937, the Springboks refused to play an all-Māori team, though several Māori played for the All Blacks. The Te Arawa tribe called for a cultural and sporting boycott, supported by most Māori, accusing the **New Zealand Rugby Football Union (NZRFU)** of putting 'cash before conscience.'

The first All Black tour of South Africa in 1928 excluded all Māori players. One, the great full-back George Nepia, later wrote, *'the whole of New Zealand was indignant at this deference to apartheid'*,[28] while the *Akarana (Auckland) Māori Association* described the action as *'a slur on the dignity and manhood of the Māori.'*[29] But another all-'white' All Black team toured South Africa in 1949, prompting even more

DISPLAY CARDS (PROBABLY POSTED ON BUSES, TRAMS AND IN STORE WINDOWS) ADVERTISES PROTEST MEETING.

protests, especially from trade unions and cultural figures such as Kiwi writer O. E. Middleton, who said there should be no more tours until South Africa had abandoned apartheid.[30]

But the NZRFU folded to South African pressure and didn't select any Māori players to tour South Africa, excluding many great players solely based on the colour of their skin. By 1960, Aotearoa/New Zealanders started to voice their discomfort and there was public outcry when another race-based team was selected to tour South Africa. In what has been described as the true beginning of the anti-apartheid movement here, there were calls of '**No Māoris — No Tour**.' Although 160,000 Aotearoa/New Zealanders signed a petition protesting against it, and thousands marched in protest, the tour still went ahead without any Māori players. This was the largest protest against racially selected sports teams in the world at that time.[31]

By 1967 the public pressure was mounting and a proposed tour of South Africa was cancelled. This action was further supported when the U.N. called for a sporting boycott against South Africa in 1968, in order to put more pressure on the South African government. As a result, a multi-racial team was sent from Aotearoa/New Zealand to play there in 1970 although this could hardly be seen as a back-down by the South Africans: **they allowed Māori players to travel there as 'honorary whites.'** This move enraged those Aotearoa/New Zealanders who actively opposed apartheid, claiming the NZRFU had allowed the Māori players to be demeaned.[32] They believed that Aotearoa/New Zealand's continued sporting contacts with South Africa would send a signal that we accepted apartheid as lawful — and that going along with their segregated stance poisoned our own attitudes and values.

By 1972, feelings toward the issue were heating up. In the lead-up to the general election of that year, the Labour Party opposition leader, Norman Kirk, pledged not to interfere with a Springbok tour scheduled for Aotearoa/New Zealand in the following year. But after he won the election, he tried to convince the NZRFU to withdraw its invitation to South Africa, while at the same time attempting to calm the rising anti-tour disquiet. Groups such as HART (Halt All Racist Tours), an organisation first started by students at University of Auckland in 1969, had gathered force, threatening public disruption, and eventually the Police advised Kirk that if the tour went ahead it would '*engender the greatest eruption of violence this country has ever known.*'[33]

In early April, 1973, Kirk wrote to the NZRFU and told them that his government saw '*no alternative, pending selection [of players] on a genuine merit basis, to a postponement of the tour.*' Despite believing that there was still, overall, majority support for the tour, he claimed he would be '*failing in his duty*' not to '*accept the criticism and do what [he] believed to be right.*' He argued that the: '*Government was elected to govern*' and that the threat to Aotearoa/New Zealand's peace was considered

ANTI-APARTHEID GROUP **HART** AT WELLINGTON AIRPORT, 1971, PROTESTING THE ARRIVAL OF THE SOUTH AFRICAN CARDINALS SOFTBALL TEAM.

too great.[#34] Only a few days later, the rugby grandstand at Papakura was burnt down in protest.

Kirk's decision was also, in part, influenced by the fact that Christchurch was scheduled to host the 1974 Commonwealth Games and several African nations were threatening to boycott the Games if the tour went ahead. But Kirk's critics said he had given in to threats from 'rent-a-mob' activists. The National Party's new leader, Robert Muldoon, claimed a government under his leadership would welcome the Springboks *'even if there were threats of violence and civil strife.'* He said that Kirk's cancellation of the tour was *'one issue on which people will change their vote.'*

And he was proved right, with the National Party winning the next election by a landslide.

1976 saw the All Blacks again accepting an invitation to tour South Africa, but this time the rest of the world looked on, prompted by the wide-spread coverage of the deadly riots in Soweto. International criticism was gathering force, and 25 African nations showed their outrage by boycotting the 1976 Montreal Olympics, with Egypt and several others eventually joining them. In the end, over 300 competitors withdrew from the games, forcing many events to be re-scheduled or cancelled. The boycott cost Canada millions of dollars. In spite of the claim by many that sports and politics shouldn't mix, the issue was now very publicly linked on the world stage. But Robert Muldoon refused to back down, despite the damage to Aotearoa/New Zealand's international reputation and rising anti-apartheid sentiment here at home.

At the 1977 *Commonwealth Heads of State* meeting, the South African situation was discussed and the subsequent **Gleneagles Agreement** was signed by all parties. This agreement accepted that it was *'the urgent duty of each of their Governments vigorously to combat the evil of apartheid by withholding any form of support for, and by taking every practical step to discourage contact or competition by their nationals with sporting organisations, teams or sportsmen from South Africa or from any other country where sports are organised on the basis of race, colour or ethnic origin.'* Although we signed up to the Gleneagles Agreement, Muldoon still voiced his disapproval at political interference in our sporting contacts. The NZRFU took this as permission to continue and invited the Springboks to tour Aotearoa/New Zealand in 1981. The deputy prime minister contacted the NZRFU chairman, **Ces Blazey,** concerned that we would seen as condoning apartheid. But, although Robert Muldoon said he could see *'nothing but trouble coming from this',* he repeated his stance that politics should stay out of sport, and declared that *'our kith and kin'* had fought alongside the South Africans in World War II and therefore we should support them now.[37]

Swept to power in the 1975 election and returned in 1978, Muldoon was confident his backing of the tours would see him re-elected in the upcoming election at the end of 1981. Public opinion polls confirmed support for the tour, especially outside of the cities, including six important electorates he believed his party could win if he maintained his pro-tour stance. According to historian Jock Phillips,[38] Muldoon's attitudes were the same as many men of his generation, who had grown up through the 1929-1932 Depression and WWII (1939-1945) and still held onto a strong belief in the British Empire and that rugby, with its emphasis on physical strength and teamwork, was central to our culture. Phillips saw the tour as a clash between the 'old and the new New Zealand', which revealed itself in five main ways: the struggle between baby boomers and war veterans, city versus country, men versus women, black versus white, and 'Britain of the South' versus an independent Pacific nation.[39]

But, although these 'old' attitudes still held sway in the halls of power, Phillips was right: Aotearoa/New Zealand was changing. The 1970s and early 1980s saw rising levels of unemployment, wage and price freezes and increasing inflation.[40] Many Aotearoa/New Zealanders, especially among the working class, were seeing their standard of living drop and many suffered job losses from increased factory

THE GLENEAGLES AGREEMENT, 22 JULY 1981.

closures which erased jobs. Our own poor history of race relations was also starting to be more widely challenged and a new generation were fighting to have their voices heard. Divisions were widening in society and anger was rising well before the 1981 Springbok Tour. It was, however, the final spark that lit the fire. For many, the Springboks' arrival became a declaration of civil war.

1981: 'ONE, TWO THREE, FOUR, WE DON'T WANT YOUR RACIST TOUR.'

The planning to **mobilise** a nation-wide anti-tour protest against the 1981 tour began well before the Springboks set foot on our soil. The key to this was a national education campaign, designed to teach people about the injustices of apartheid and the important issues at stake.

Speaking tours by those involved in the South African struggle were organised and anti-tour groups delivered thousands of leaflets to letterboxes. **Trevor Richards, founder of HART (Halt All Racist Tours)**, and many others travelled the country and brought people together to set up local anti-tour groups. Fundraising drives took place to support such actions and letter writing campaigns were started.

A series of rallies, including those held on 1 May and 3 July, resulted in tens of thousands of people marching in cities and towns up and down the country. These were the biggest demonstrations Aotearoa/New Zealand had ever seen, and prepared protesters for direct actions planned to take place once the Springboks arrived.

The anti-tour protesters weren't the only groups preparing in advance for the tour. Police started planning in September 1980, with a top-level get-together held at Police National Headquarters, headed

SOME OF THE MAIN ANTI TOUR GROUPS:

AUCKLAND COMMITTEE ON RACISM AND DISCRIMINATION (ACCORD)

CITIZENS ALL BLACK TOUR ASSOCIATION (CABTA) – started in the late 1950s.

CITIZENS ASSOCIATION FOR RACIAL EQUALITY (CARE) – formed in Auckland in 1964.

CATHOLICS AGAINST THE TOUR (CATT)

COALITION TO OPPOSE THE SPRINGBOK TOUR (COST) – a Wellington-based group.

HALT ALL RACISTS TOURS (HART) – set up by Trevor Richards of the NZ University Students Association in 1969. It became an umbrella group including CARE and a range of student, church, Māori and other Left-leaning groups.

MĀORI ORGANISATION ON HUMAN RIGHTS (MAHR) – led by Tamatekapua Poata

MOBILISATION TO STOP THE TOUR (MOST) – an Auckland-based group.

NATIONAL ANTI-APARTHEID COUNCIL (NAAC)

NGĀ TAMATOA – anti-racism group made up of young Māori, who also campaigned on issues such as loss of land and language and Treaty breaches.

SCHOOL STUDENTS AGAINST THE TOUR (SSAT) – (secondary school students)

STUDENTS AGAINST THE TOUR (SSAT) – (tertiary students)

WOMEN AGAINST THE TOUR (WATT)

PRO-TOUR GROUPS:

NEW ZEALAND RUGBY FOOTBALL UNION (NZRFU)

SOCIETY FOR THE PROTECTION OF INDIVIDUAL RIGHTS (SPIR)

TOUR TIMELINE

12th September: 1980: New Zealand Rugby Football Union (NZRFU) formally invites the South African rugby team to tour New Zealand.

1st May 1981: First organised mass protests take place throughout the country. Numbers were estimated at around 75,000 people.

14th May 1981: The Prime Minister Robert Muldoon is presented with an ultimatum by the Commonwealth to cancel the tour or lose hosting rights to Commonwealth Finance Ministers Conference due to take place in Auckland.

3rd July 1981: Second of the mass protests held throughout country.

10th July 1981: The NZRFU meet for the last time to decide whether the tour should proceed **or be cancelled.**

19th July 1981: The Springboks arrive in Aotearoa/New Zealand, landing at Auckland airport.

22nd July 1981: First game played - Springboks vs Poverty Bay in Gisborne. South Africa wins 24 to 6.

25th July 1981: Springboks vs Waikato game in Hamilton called off following a pitch invasion by protestors.

27th July 1981: The government says it won't back down in the face of violent protests and promises the police the assistance of the NZ army if required.

29th July 1981: Anti-tour protests outside Parliament reach a new level of violence in an event which becomes known as the "Battle of Molesworth Street". Springboks play Taranaki at New Plymouth and win 34 to 9.

31st July 1981: The Prime Minister threatens to call a snap election if anti-tour violence continues to escalate.

1st August 1981: Springboks vs Manawatu in Palmerston North. South Africa win 31 to 19.

2nd August 1981: In his speech at the annual National Party Conference, Robert Muldoon claims that the extreme-left wing agitators have taken over the anti-tour protest movement.

11th August 1981: Springboks vs Otago in Dunedin. South Africa win 17 to 13.

13th August 1981: The grandstand at Rugby Park in Christchurch is destroyed by fire in a suspected arson attack after a Springboks training session at the ground.

15th August 1981: First test played in Christchurch. NZ win 14 to 9.

19th August 1981: Springboks vs South Canterbury at Timaru cancelled for 'security' reasons.

29th August 1981: Second test played in Wellington. South Africa win 24 to 12.

12th September 1981: Third test played in Auckland. This day also commemorated the death of South African activist Steve Biko, who was murdered while in police custody. NZ win 25 to 22.

13th September 1981: Springboks depart New Zealand

by Chief Superintendent Brian Davies. A policing budget of $2.2 million was announced by Prime Minister Robert Muldoon on December 15, 1980.[#42] This resulted in the formation of an elite police task force, designed to manage the non-violent disruptions promised by anti-tour groups.

Three special elite police forces were trained, the Red, White and Blue Squads. Armed with long-batons, they underwent five day courses, one full day spent on how to wield the batons. Made of plastic, this type of baton was originally used as a martial-arts weapon and the training sessions were led by a martial arts master. They practiced *'draws, spins, punches, chops, blocks, extraction, running arm-locks and hand-cuff arm-locks.'* [#42]

Most Aotearoa/New Zealanders had never seen the long-baton used in such a way before, and the training was supposed to be kept secret. But copies of the training documents were leaked to HART and shared at their national meeting on July 11th. Auckland's leader of HART, **John Minto**, wrote to Police Commissioner **Bob Walton**, asking him to confirm the long-baton training. This leaking of information was a two-way street, however. The police planted informants inside the main protest groups and there was one documented instance of a protest leader alerting police to a 'fringe' member of HART who stated several times he would shoot at least one Springbok before the team left Aotearoa/New Zealand.

THE TOUR BEGINS: JULY 19TH 1981 [#43]

The Springboks arrived at Auckland International Airport on July 19th, a drizzly Sunday afternoon. 2,000 protesters met them, with 378 police there as well. Some of the protesters tore down the wire security fence and rushed onto the tarmac. Down in Wellington, at the same time, a simultaneous action was taking place. Around 200 protesters filled the domestic terminal, with 50 or so running out onto the runway to block it. Both police and Air New Zealand were taken by surprise. Later, the Springboks were taken to Poho-o-Rawiri marae in Gisborne for an official welcome.

What now unfolded over the course of the tour was a nation-wide campaign to stop the Springboks playing. Each venue where a game was scheduled became a centre for protest, backed by other synchronised events all around the country, designed to stretch police resources, and gain media attention and public support.

POLICE COMMISSIONER, BOB WALTON

HART'S AUCKLAND LEADER, JOHN MINTO

GAME ON: GISBORNE, WEDNESDAY 22 JULY

Even before the first starting whistle, anti-tour protesters had dealt this game its opening blow. The night before, a hired Landrover smashed through the fence and hurtled around the park, scattering broken glass onto the field. Police arrested the perpetrators, but were still on high alert the next morning after receiving a tip that the protesters intended to use a light plane to drop parachuted protesters onto the field to disrupt play. They insisted Civil Aviation put a 'no fly' zone in place but no aeroplane appeared.

Meanwhile, as the Springboks stepped out to play Poverty Bay, tour supporters and anti-tour protesters faced-off for the first time. Protesters wrestled to demolish the perimeter fence while umbrella-wielding rugby supporters fought them off. The scenes were described as muddy and chaotic. The following year, police admitted that the intensity of the protest had surprised most of them and it was clear things were only going to get worse. They were right.

Conveniently, Prime Minister Robert Muldoon flew overseas for a ten day trip hours after the first game. While at home a civil war was unfolding, Muldoon was off to attend the royal wedding of Prince Charles and Lady Diana Spencer.

GAME OFF: HAMILTON, SATURDAY 25 JULY

Police stepped up their numbers for the game at Hamilton's Rugby Park on 25 July: 535 police were on hand, with the Red Squad hiding below the grandstand should things turn ugly. But a further 240 police were delayed by fog at Hamilton airport, only arriving by bus after the drama was over. They had anticipated a thousand protesters; instead 4000 converged on the park.

ANTI-TOUR PROTESTERS PULL DOWN FENCE AT HAMILTON'S RUGBY PARK

Already protesters in Hamilton had let the Springboks know they were not wanted there. The night before the game, a group of over 500 people marched, chanting and singing freedom songs, to the Ambassador Hotel where the Springboks were staying. Then, on the day of the match, 400 protesters (of the total 4000) demolished the boundary fence in a matter of seconds just before kick-off, rushing onto the pitch. Arms linked, they stood at the centre of the field and chanted *'The whole world's watching'* and *'Shame, shame, shame.'* Their action was broadcast live around the world, the group made up of a cross-section of Aotearoa/New Zealand society.

At 3.15pm, after the police had undertaken a long negotiation with protest leaders and made slow progress in arresting those on the field (50 arrests over the course of an hour), Police Commissioner Bob Walton officially called off the game. Back in a South African jail, Nelson Mandela (who would be elected South Africa's President after the fall of apartheid) heard of the cancellation and said it was *'as if the sun had come out.'* Only much later it was revealed that the reason for Walton's move was not only the on-field protest, but news that protester

TOP: REVEREND GEORGE ARMSTRONG ADDRESSES POLICE AT A PROTEST

LEFT: RUGBY SUPPORTERS AND ANTI-TOUR PROTESTERS CLASH

Pat McQuarrie was flying towards Hamilton in a plane stolen from Taupo, with a plan to crash this aircraft into the main stand. But when McQuarrie heard news of the cancellation via a portable radio he turned around and abandoned the plan.

For many in the anti-tour movement, this day was triumph. For rugby fans, the cancellation was an outrage and they soon made their feelings known. Skirmishes broke out and protesters were battered by objects hurled from the crowd. As both groups swarmed out of Rugby Park, further violence erupted. The rugby fans attacked the protesters and the protestors fought back. Cars and vans used to transport injured protesters were attacked, shop windows with rugby-themed displays were smashed, cameras recording the riot were snatched away and broken, beer cans and crates were thrown as missiles. Even after the worst of the riot had died down, protest leaders, including John Minto, were attacked in their homes and badly beaten.

As a result of this riot, which police took as a humiliation, their tactics hardened. They poured more resources into their efforts and were promised the help of the NZ Army if required. The final bill across all government departments trebled to $7.2 million. [#44]

The hardening of tactics and positions was also reflected in the formation of the **Patu Squad**, a protester group particularly prepared to stand-up to the Red Squad. According to Te Ara, the Encyclopedia of New Zealand, *'the Patu Squad in Auckland was led by Māori activists* **Ripeka Evans**, **Donna Awatere** *and* **Hone Harawira**. *It had a core of around 100 members, mostly Māori. While the squad represented Māori opposition to the tour, there was overlap with other protest groups such as HART.'* [#45] Some of the members of the **Polynesian Panthers** (see the chapter on the Dawn Raids), and **Ngā Tamatoa**, were also involved. Several of the Patu Squad were arrested and later imprisoned for inciting riots and grievous bodily harm. **Will 'Ilolahia**, one of the founders of the Polynesian Panthers, was also among those charged for inciting riots. South African Bishop Desmond Tutu was called as a defence witness and 'Ilolahia (among others) was found not guilty. [#46] It is reported that when Nelson Mandela came to Aotearoa/New Zealand in 1995 he wanted to meet the Patu Squad,[#427] to thank them for their support.

THE BATTLE OF MOLESWORTH STREET: WELLINGTON, WEDNESDAY 29 JULY

Also known by some as 'The Night of the Batons', this protest marked a real turning point in terms of both police brutality and a hardening of protester resolve.

On the evening after the Springboks played against the Taranaki team in New Plymouth, around 2000 protesters met outside Parliament in Wellington, with a plan to march up Molesworth Street towards the home of the South African Consulate-General.

The mood was cheerful, the cancellation of the game at Hamilton buoying the protesters confidence. Across the world, Robert Muldoon was at that very moment attending the royal wedding at St Paul's Cathedral, London, and talk of the wedding also helped to lighten the mood. As the marchers moved off, many women, children and the elderly moved to the front to ensure police restraint.

According to later news reports,[#48] Inspector Bert Hill, using a megaphone, warned the protesters: *'Would you please not go out on to Molesworth Street.'* But, despite five lines of police blocking the march's proposed route outside Parliament's main gates, protest marshals declared they would keep going and the march surged forward. Police stood their ground as crowds further behind forced those in

 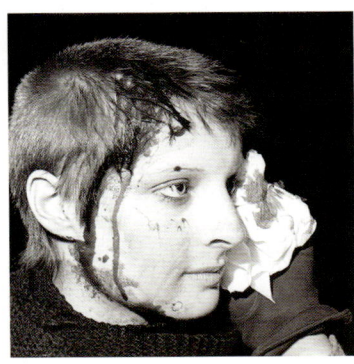

front directly into the police line. The police took this as a deliberate refusal to obey them and pushed back to the cry of 'Move, move, move', attacking those in their path with short batons. A Dominion journalist, two metres from the front line, reported hearing no order for batons to be used.

Stunned protesters – some covered in blood – reeled away in horror and confusion. Chants of 'Shame, shame, shame' broke out and a group of protesters swung back into the city, heading for the central police station to lay assault charges. #49

Police would later claim they had been pushed, kicked, and had their ties torn off, and that they were acting in self-defence. Deputy Chief Inspector Peter Faulkner maintained the batons were drawn for twenty seconds at the most. But the damage was done. Photos of battered protesters, including a 16-year-old high student, Karen Brough, bleeding from the head, shocked and outraged the nation.

By now the issue had so split opinions, family members refused to speak to others with differing points of view, friendships broke up, workplaces became verbal battle grounds, and pubs became potential war zones.

LEFT: BATON-WIELDING POLICE AND ANTI-TOUR PROTESTERS CLASH IN MOLESWORTH ST, WELLINGTON

RIGHT: 16 YEAR OLD HIGH SCHOOL STUDENT KAREN BROUGH WAS HIT BY A POLICE BATON ON HER HEAD, BACK AND ARMS

'I was 21 and went to the protest with my younger sister and older brother, not expecting trouble. As we stood around at Parliament waiting for the march to begin, everyone was joking about the royal wedding in England, which was taking place at the same time. There were lots of old and young people in the crowd. We started marching up Molesworth Street when suddenly those at the front turned and started running back towards us, crushing us and screaming, some with blood streaming down their faces. My sister was so scared she jumped onto my back and I ran with her until we were clear of the march. I've never felt so terrified. Even now, I've never fully recovered my trust of the police.' Molesworth Street, first-hand witness account.

Later in Parliament, Mangere MP David Lange (later Prime Minister) would mock Muldoon, who was still away at the royal wedding: *'There may be garden parties in London, but it is no garden party here.'* Lange criticised the Government for putting police into the position of needing this combat style of policing. *'If the Government unleashes the tiger and then cries "Wolf!" there will be a backlash.'*

In response, on 31 July, Prime Minister Robert Muldoon threatened to call a snap election.

MANAWATU MARCHES: PALMERSTON NORTH, SATURDAY 1 AUGUST

As cars, buses and vans full of protesters converged on Palmerston North, where the Springboks would play the Manawatu side, the police tried new tactics devised after the Hamilton pitch invasion.

Barbed-wire barriers were erected, 2m high and 3m wide, reinforced with large rubbish skips, to block marchers from anywhere near the venue. More than 1,100 police were brought in and Auckland's Red Squad, decked out in full riot gear, held the line against protesters, many of whom wore crash helmets and extra padding. Though a lot of noise and banner-waving occurred, the police kept the protesters away from the rugby grounds. But though the police claimed this as their victory, the Red Squad's behaviour prompted much hostility, and their reputation for ruthless viciousness grew, with many protesters clubbed by batons before arrest.

In a speech at the National Party Conference on 2 August, Muldoon claimed that 'extreme-left wing agitators' had taken over the protest movement. To back this claim, he released to the press a list of 20 supposed 'subversives' involved in the protests (including Māori 'radicals'), prepared by the SIS, Aotearoa/New Zealand's internal intelligence agency [50]. The SIS was later successfully sued for publicising incorrect information in the dossier. [51]

FIRE! FIRE! CHRISTCHURCH, THURSDAY 13 AUGUST

Two days after the Springboks played Otago in Dunedin, and two days before the first rugby test was due to be played in Christchurch, the grandstand at Rugby Park, Christchurch, (where the Springboks were to train) was destroyed by fire. It was believed the fire was deliberately lit by anti-tour protesters. No arrests were made.

BOOM! CHRISTCHURCH, FRIDAY 14 AUGUST

On the night of 14 August, a bomb blast woke residents near Lancaster Park, Christchurch, where the first test was to be played the following day. Police confirmed it was caused by an 'explosive device" placed near the park's perimeter but said it had caused no damage or injuries. Barbed-wire barricades remained in place. [52]

THE FIRST TEST MATCH – ALL BLACKS VS SPRINGBOKS: CHRISTCHURCH, SATURDAY 15 AUGUST

On the day, 1473 police patrolled Lancaster Park and the seventeen protesters who ran onto the pitch were *'savagely dispatched.'* [53] Geoff Chapple, in his book *1981: The Tour* said of the atmosphere in Christchurch at the time, it was as if *'some dark and cataclysmic star had begun to descend over the city.'* Chapple described the moments when the Red Squad went after protesters who made it to the pitch:

'The batons thudded. People were injured and screaming. Heads were bleeding again. A man in his 40s was staggering around with his teeth punched out.' [54] Rugby fans cheered on the Red Squad and pummelled protesters with anything they could find

INJURED PROTESTER ON RINTOUL STREET, WELLINGTON.

to throw. One policeman recalled that it was 'sheer luck' no one was killed that day.[55] The All Blacks won the first test 14–9.

CANCELLED! TIMARU, WEDNESDAY 19 AUGUST

The game scheduled between the Springboks and South Canterbury at Timaru's Fraser Park was cancelled, police arguing the ground was too difficult to guard.[56] However, sports writer Don Cameron suggested the game was called off *'so that the police could rest many of their over-worked force.'*[57]

A CAPITAL BATTLEFIELD - THE SECOND TEST: WELLINGTON, SATURDAY 29 AUGUST

Early on the morning of the second test between the Springboks and the All Blacks, 7000 protesters gathered in the capital city. Despite the 1611 police on duty, concern for the Springboks' safety was so grave they spent the previous night sleeping under the grandstand. On the day, a further 37 officers from a special police surveillance squad, along with another intelligence group of 14, infiltrated the crowds.

Protest groups blocked the motorway exits into the city, as well as road and pedestrian access to Athletic Park, forcing police to form human wedges to escort rugby fans through. Fighting between fans and protesters broke out and batons were again used. Television coverage was also disrupted.

'I recall a wet afternoon marshalling about a hundred mostly middle-aged people happily singing "Kumbaya" in the middle of the Hutt Road. The cop in charge approached me and the other marshal and said very pleasantly: "Look guys I want this road clear. I haven't got enough forces to arrest you all. But there's no TV cameras anywhere in sight, so if you don't piss off in two minutes we'll just wade in with some heavy stuff, okay?" We gathered up our singers and slowly marched back to town, taking as much time as we could. There was a big argument that night as to whether we'd not been staunch enough.'
Don Franks [58]

'ALL HELL BREAKS LOOSE' - THE THIRD AND FINAL TEST: AUCKLAND, SATURDAY 12 SEPTEMBER

On the day commemorating South African activist Steve Biko's brutal murder in custody, this final test at Eden Park was to prove the bloodiest and most violent of all the clashes. Police numbered 2,134, sandwiched between thousands of protesters and rugby fans, and they would later describe what unfolded as a full-blown riot. Missile-throwing fans and protesters battled with police, who reported: *'The items thrown . . .comprised of rotten eggs, evil smelling unidentified substance, bottles, cans, broken field pipes, volcanic rock, metal bars, wooden palings, incendiary devices (including phosphorus flares), steel bars.'*

Protesters were divided into squads, with women and children kept separate from the most actively disruptive protesters. One of them was named the 'Biko squad', in commemoration of Biko's death.

Over 200 protesters were arrested and dozens were injured, including numerous injuries among the police as well. A group of protesters in Dominion Road dressed as clowns were brutally beaten by three Red Squad members, one of the clowns left unconscious, in what became one of the most serious allegations of unnecessary police force. Inquiries into the incident would see police close ranks, especially among members of the Red Squad, and the perpetrators went unpunished.

Journalist Pekka Paavonpera described standing on Dominion Road at the time and seeing several police break away from their group. *'They came running towards me and I thought, shit, this is going to be me. Then they saw these clowns and something set them off, so they headed for the clowns.'*[#59]

Paavonpera also described the police as wearing full-face helmets, with no identification badges showing as they drew out their batons.

*'They were vicious, raining blows all over them. The girl, she was on the ground and they just kept going. I ran over . . . and yelled out, "Stop it, for f***'s sake, stop it . . . one of the [police] . . . took a swing at me and missed. The other two just kept on beating. . . I was convinced the girl was dead. I thought they had busted her neck.'*

An inquiry into this incident would last right through until March 1982, with no individual police being identified. Eventually the clowns sued the police department, and were awarded a payment of $10,000 each. In 2001, one of the clowns spoke to a

A CESSNA AIRCRAFT LOW OVER EDEN PARK IN AN ATTEMPT TO STOP THE ALL BLACKS V SPRINGBOKS' THIRD AND FINAL RUGBY TEST MATCH.

reporter from the NZ Herald. *'At the time, we all lost faith in the justice system, but I guess in hindsight we realised that the police were caught between a rock and a hard place.'*[#60]

The running battle between police, protesters and fans was not the only drama to unfold that day. A Cessna aircraft, flown by one of the protesters, swooped over Eden Park and dropped flour and smoke bombs into the crowd and over the pitch. All Black Gary Knight was hit by a flour bomb and knocked over.

At the other end of the country, too, a group of six protesters from Dunedin sabotaged the TV transmitter on Mt Studholme. 58,000 viewers in the Timaru, Waimate, Fairlie and South Canterbury area lost TV1 and TV2 for 80 minutes. At the same time, 60% of the southern half of the South Island had their live broadcast cut when protesters also took out the transmitter at Mt Cargill.[#61]

TOP: POLICE ATTACKED PROTESTERS DRESSED AS CLOWNS IN AUCKLAND. AN INQUIRY INTO THE INCIDENT WOULD LATER BE HELD AND EVENTUALLY THE CLOWNS WOULD SUE THE POLICE

LEFT: ALL BLACK PROP, GARY KNIGHT, IS FELLED BY A FLOUR BOMB.

NELSON MANDELA

Amandla Ngawethu! Power to us!

"No one is born hating another person because of the colour of his skin, or his background, or his religion. People must learn to hate, and if they can learn to hate, they can be taught to love, for love comes more naturally to the human heart than its opposite."

NELSON MANDELA AND F.W DE KLERK.

Remarkably, the final test was played and the All Blacks won 25-22. The day after the Springboks flew out of Auckland. In the 56 days they had been in the country, over 2000 New Zealanders had been arrested and the bitterness and divisions spurred by the protests took years to heal. Robert Muldoon never publicly voiced any regret over the tour.

ANTI-TOUR CONTAGION: NEXT THE US MAKES ITS FEELINGS KNOWN

After their tumultuous tour of Aotearoa/New Zealand, the Springboks flew to the US to play. Threats of riots caused officials in Los Angeles, Chicago, New York City and Rochester to cancel proposed games there and, where games *were* played, protesters made their feelings plain. A pipe bomb set off outside the headquarters of the Eastern Rugby Union caused no injuries but $50,000 worth of damage. [62]

WHAT DID ALL THIS MEAN AND WHAT DID IT ACHIEVE?

SOUTH AFRICA

There is now no doubt that Aotearoa/New Zealanders' anti-apartheid stance during the 1981 Springbok Tour, and afterwards, gave encouragement and hope to those in South Africa fighting its oppressive system.

But back in South Africa, the repression of anti-apartheid activists continued to increase after 1981. Now, more and more, however, South Africa was isolated internationally for its racist policies, and support for the imprisoned Mandela, who had become a symbol for the resistance, steadily grew. By the mid-1980s, small moves had been made to ease some of the more 'petty' apartheid laws, and President Botha warned 'white' South Africans to *'adapt or die.'* [63]

After the death of Botha in 1989, **F.W de Klerk** succeeded him as president. In his opening address to parliament in February 1990, he announced he would repeal discriminatory laws and lift the 30-year ban on anti-apartheid groups such as Mandela's ANC. Nine days later, Mandela was released after over 27 years in jail.

In 1991 South Africa's apartheid legislation was finally abolished. The country held its first fully free election in 1994 and the ANC won 62.65% of the vote. Mandela was sworn in as President, with de Klerk and **Thabo Mbeki** appointed deputy presidents. The anniversary of this election, 27th of April, is now celebrated in South Africa with a public holiday known as **Freedom Day**. In 1993 both Mandela and de Klerk were awarded Nobel Peace Prizes.[64]

In a highly innovative and inspirational move, Mandela's government set up the **Truth and Reconciliation Commission**, designed to give those who had inflicted racial violence a chance to confess and make amends. It was seen as an act of cleansing, allowing the wound of apartheid to be lanced and drained, to leave the country healthier as it moved forwards. This process lasted until 2002 and, although it wasn't without flaws, it was viewed as a successful process overall and has since been used by other countries around the world who hope to heal post-conflict communities.

Sadly, this didn't mean that life in South Africa miraculously improved for every citizen. The process has continued to be complex, fraught with difficulties, corruption and violent opposing interests, particularly after Mandela was replaced by Jacob Zuma as President. As this is being written, Zuma (now retired) is in the process of being charged for corruption during his time in power.[65] It is still uncertain how much conflict this will spark within the country but, as one commentator said, it is a real test of whether South Africa has reached maturity and can reject the corruption and power-grabbing evident in so many of the other repressive leaders still in power. All this aside, it is still worth celebrating that the core apartheid legislation which tens of thousands of Aotearoa/New Zealanders fought to overturn is now the stuff of history.

'The people of New Zealand played a crucial role in the international campaign against apartheid. I wish to express our gratitude for that generous support.' [66] Nelson Mandela, during a visit to Aotearoa/New Zealand in his role as President of South Africa in 1995.

AOTEAROA/NEW ZEALAND

But what about here in Aotearoa/New Zealand? The immediate aftermath of the tour at home saw courts tied up with police cases against anti-tour protesters for the rest of the year, in a nation still reeling at what had taken place. Pro or anti positions continued to be tightly held, with the ethics of rugby sporting contact again in the news in 1986, when an 'unofficial' rugby tour of South Africa took place. The official All Black tour planned for 1985 was cancelled after a legal ruling but a rebel team, called the *NZ Cavaliers*, found themselves with far less support than they expected. On their return to Aotearoa/New Zealand the rebel players were barred from the next two All Black test matches.[67] No other sporting contact took place between Aotearoa/New Zealand and South Africa until the end of apartheid.

HOW DID ALL THIS IMPACT ON AOTEAROA/NEW ZEALAND SOCIETY?

Perhaps the most significant consequence was the spotlight the protests put on our own race relations here at home. For generations Aotearoa/New Zealanders had claimed we had the best race relations in the world, despite lacking real evidence to support this. As the Tour protests focused on attacking racism, and Māori joined the cause, more and more questions were asked about our own shabby human rights record in relation to Māori and Pacific Islanders, and our failure to first acknowledge and then to stamp out racism. Groups like Ngā Tamatoa and the Polynesian Panthers, and activists such as Syd Jackson, Tamatekapua Poata, Donna Awatere and Hone Harawira, John Minto and Trevor

OPINION ON THE SPRINGBOK TOUR, JULY 1981

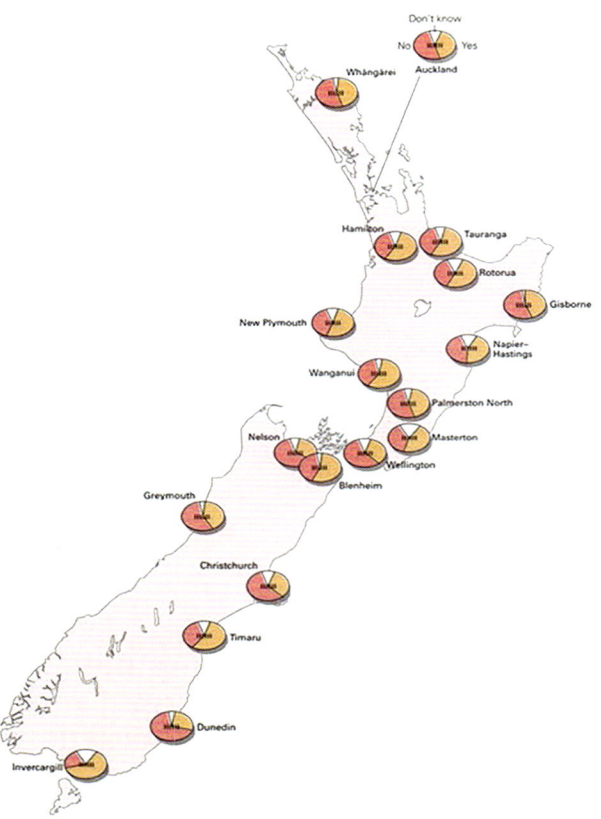

REGIONAL RESPONSES TO THE QUESTION 'SHOULD THE SPRINGBOK RUGBY TEAM HAVE COME TO NEW ZEALAND?'
RED = NO
ORANGE = YES

Richards (among many), pointed to the injustices Māori and Pacific Islanders still faced here. Perhaps for the first time, 'ordinary' Pākehā Aotearoa/New Zealanders began to understand the issues and the need for real change.

John Minto summed this up, saying, *'I think one of the critical things that happened as a result of that Tour and the protests, had in fact a bigger effect within New Zealand than a lasting effect within South Africa. But what it did was things like the Waitangi Tribunal, up until then they could only look at issues which were new grievances, but after the Tour and that whole upwelling of debate and arguments about racism here, people started to realise you can't protest against racism 6,000 miles away when it's right here in your country… and a few years later the Tribunal was able to look at past grievances. There was a big movement in recognising racism in our own country and giving Maori a place to stand in their own land.'* [#68]

Trevor Richards agreed, noting how this new understanding of our own inbuilt racism took effect: *'We built a movement that crossed generational and class boundaries and helped shift New Zealand into a different national and international consciousness… ultimately [the issues] were more about us than they were about South Africa.'* [#69]

Another unanticipated consequence saw the reputation of rugby so badly damaged that other sports started to be more heavily promoted in schools. As a result, sports such as soccer, hockey, rowing and tennis suddenly grew more popular. [#70] Many people's attitude towards the police — and authority in general — took a hit as the result of the violent clashes seen throughout the tour, especially those who confronted the Blue and Red Squads. As cases such as the clown-bashing incident dragged on through the courts, with no one seeming to take responsibility for the police actions, many questioned the processes and lack of accountability and justice. Others who had come face to face with the baton-swinging riot squads found their level of trust in the police so eroded it would never be fully repaired.

On a positive note, a new generation of Aotearoa/New Zealanders now had proof that concerted public action could make change both here and abroad. As with all the other topics covered in this book, this chapter of our history helped us to view ourselves as an independent nation, prepared to stand up for the human rights and justice issues we believed in. Since the Tour, our culture has been enriched by continued creative exploration of those times through film, documentary, music, plays, photos, writing and artworks. Merata Mita's documentary *Patu!, for instance,* is an invaluable and amazing record of the protests. [#71]

It has been said that the 1981 Springbok Tour was our 'growing up' moment. But perhaps it is better described as our 'adolescent' moment, when we broke away from 'Mother England' and pushed at all the boundaries in search of our unique identity. Perhaps our real 'adult' moment is still to come, when we stop paying mere lip-service to race relations here at home and finally, properly, address the inequities in our treatment of tangata whenua and our Pacific cousins, who still languish at the bottom of all our health and well-being statistics.

Imagine if the tens of thousands of people who stood up for the downtrodden in South Africa during the apartheid years, did the same for those still suffering back here in Aotearoa/New Zealand?

As Nelson Mandela said:
'As long as poverty, injustice and gross inequality persist in our world, none of us can truly rest.'

KEY CHANGE-MAKERS

Go online or check out your library for more on each of these change-makers — people prepared to put themselves in the public eye to fight for others' rights.

NELSON MANDELA

DESMOND TUTU · STEVE BIKO · JOHN MINTO

NORMAN KIRK · DONNA AWATERE · TREVOR RICHARDS

RIPEKA EVANS · SYD JACKSON · WILL 'ILOLAHIA

RACISM NEVER SLEEPS

THE DAWN RAIDS

It's easy to be shocked and outraged by the racism of South Africa's old apartheid system, but what happens when we see such racism stirred up in our own backyard? In the early 1970s we witnessed just that with what became known as Dawn Raids where the police could legally decend in the early hours of the morning with tracking dogs. Catching people in their homes, half asleep and vulnerable and fearful, Police would challenge people to provide proof of their right to be here.

A LITTLE BACKGROUND FIRST:

In the years after WWII, Aotearoa/New Zealand enjoyed a period of huge economic growth, which left employers desperate to fill the many jobs created by this. By the 1960s, this boom saw labour shortages in many factory and unskilled jobs. To fill the gaps, people from other Pacific nations were encouraged to leave their homes and migrate with their families as part of a labour work scheme. They were promised a new and better life here, with greater work opportunities than they had at home.

Many Tongan, Samoan, and Fijian families made the move, along with people from Niue, Tokelau, and the Cook Islands, who are legally Aotearoa/New Zealand citizens. Most, by far, settled in Auckland.

At the time of the *1945 Census of Population and Dwellings*, there were fewer than 2,200 other Pacific Island people living in Aotearoa/New Zealand.[#73] In 1968, the television show '*Compass*' reported that Auckland had become the '*unofficial capital of Polynesia*',[#74] with an estimated 20,000 people from other Pacific nations making the city their home. From 1961 to 1971, Pacific Island populations here rose from 12,000 to 48,000,[#75] and by the time of the 1976 Census there were almost 65,700 Pacific Island people living in Aotearoa/New Zealand , making up 2.1% of the total population.[#76] This figure reached 90,000 by 1981.[#77] They came for the job opportunities and hopes for a more prosperous life for their families. These were also seen as opportunities for their children to have education and choice over their future vocation.

GEORGE JACKSON/SOLEDAD BROTHERS SOLIDARITY MARCH TO THE U.S. CONSULATE, 3 MARCH 1972.

KEYWORDS

Amnesty: an official pardon (or temporary pardon) for people who have been convicted of political offences.

Assimilate/assimilation: absorb and integrate (people, ideas, or culture) into a dominant society or culture.

Assumption: a thing that is accepted as true or as certain to happen, without proof.

Criminalising: turning someone into a criminal by making their activities illegal.

Deportation: the act of expelling a foreigner from a country.

Egalitarian: the principle that all people are equal and deserve equal rights and opportunities.

Ingrained: a firmly fixed or established habit, belief, or attitude; difficult to change.

Institutional racism: racial discrimination that has become established as normal behaviour within a society or organisation.

Migrants: a person who moves from one place to another in order to find work or better living conditions.

Minority: a small group of people within a community or country, differing from the main population in race, religion, language, or political beliefs.

Persecuted: someone subjected to hostility and severe ill-treatment, especially because of their race or political or religious beliefs.

Recession (economic): a period of economic decline

Short-term Work Permits: allows you to work and live somewhere for a fixed, short, time

Stereotypes: a widely held, fixed and oversimplified image or idea of a particular type of person or thing.

Unconscious Bias: Stereotypes we believe without being aware of it.

Victimising: singling someone (or a group) out for cruel or unjust treatment.

As many as 25,000 permanent **migrants** came from the Pacific region between 1972 and 1978, making people from Pacific nations the third largest group of migrants behind those who came from Britain and Australia. Many more came on short-term work permits, here with the goal to earn extra money for their families and then return home.

A VISIBLE MINORITY

Arriving in a country that has a different language and cultural practices from your own brings with it countless difficulties. For most migrants and refugees, one of the easiest ways to learn how to fit into the culture of a new country is to seek support from others within their own culture who have already made the move. As a result, many Pacific Island families ended up living together in Auckland's poorest, most run-down inner suburbs of that time — Ponsonby, Newton, Grey Lynn, Freemans Bay and Parnell, these days known as Auckland's wealthier suburbs.

Back then they mainly consisted of dilapidated old villas and workers' cottages with no hot water or inside toilets. In fact, a 1971 report [78] found that 21% of houses rented to Māori or people from Pacific nations had no piped water supply at all, 17% had no hand basins and 50% had no safe [79] for food storage, let alone a refrigerator.

As well as this desire for community, Pacific migrants often found themselves forced into this sub-standard housing by racist landlords who were not compelled to rent them decent housing, and by lack of money, due to filling the low paid jobs that Kiwis weren't prepared to do. While their wages still far exceeded what they could earn back at home, the higher costs of living here (and the common practice of sending money back to support family in the Islands) left many families caught in a poverty trap, struggling to make ends meet. Many worked two or three jobs just to keep afloat. Many still do. Already victims of racist attitudes from landlords, Pacific Island migrants also suffered from more widespread and **ingrained** racism. One of the most destructive attitudes was the notion that those who arrived here should culturally **assimilate** – in other words, reject their own customs and language to conform with the majority Pākehā customs and attitudes. Rather than recognising that language barriers and vastly different cultural values are bound to draw together people who understand and share a culture (especially when they're made to feel like outsiders), this so-called lack of assimilation was viewed as a problem. To make matters worse, their 'difference' was highlighted by the fact that they were a very *visible minority* [80] i.e. they didn't look like Pākehā New Zealanders. While migrants from Europe and North America, for instance, could blend into the 'accepted' colour palette (white), people from Pacific nations could not.

'FIT IN OR GET OUT'

As the economic boom started to slow, Pacific Island migrants found themselves blamed for a variety of social problems. *'In order for New Zealanders to blame Pacific Islanders for taking New Zealanders' jobs and houses, there was an **implicit assumption** of what a New Zealander was and that Pacific Islanders in New Zealand collectively fell outside of this definition.'* [81] What this really means is that it's easier to blame the 'other' than to look critically at our own behaviours. If we think about the labelling of people in South Africa (or any other point in history when a certain group is **persecuted**, like Jews, for instance, or Muslims), this claim that they are somehow 'lesser' human beings forms the justification of most human rights abuses over the course of human existence. Like members in different races being lumped together as 'black' or 'coloured' under apartheid, people from all corners of the Pacific found themselves lumped together as 'Pacific Islanders'.

'When I first stepped on the shore of New Zealand, the first thing that made me react was that I was called an 'Islander'. I always regarded myself as a Māori in the Cook Islands.' Reverend Ta Upu Rae, 1977.

It's important to remember that the dominant myth about Aotearoa/New Zealand at this time was that we lived in an **egalitarian**, multicultural paradise, where everyone was equally valued and got on. But in the early 1970s, a common theme started appearing in letters to newspapers and in newspaper editorials: '*Fit In Or Get Out.*' [83] This attitude spread through many parts of society, with 62% of Auckland company managers in 1978 also agreeing, saying that people from Pacific nations should reject their traditional cultural practices and adopt Aotearoa/New Zealand 's 'local lifestyle.' [84] Between 1972 and 1978, a total of 130 'anti-Pacific Islander' letters were published in just two newspapers, with another 28 complaining letters written to the Minister of Immigration. [85] Complaints ranged from lack of assimilation, through contributing to crime, unemployment and housing shortages, to breeding too fast, clogging hospitals, bringing disease and being 'overstayers' [86] (those without permission to stay in the country indefinitely).

One editorial in the national *Herald* newspaper declared: *'they tend to congregate, if not segregate themselves, in decadent areas which could become ghettos if action was not taken.'* [87]

Vaiao Ala 'ima Etueti, co-chair of the *Auckland Pacific Island Advisory Council*, countered: *'As a rule Aucklanders, Pākehās, blatantly refuse to accept the fact that this is a South Pacific country, Auckland is a South Pacific city and the Pacific Islanders are here to stay. A large and very vocal section of the population would like us to 'kill' our cultural differences and peculiarities and become 'Kiwis.'* [88]

THE EFFECTS OF COLONISATION AND INSTITUTIONAL RACISM:

The targeted **criminalising** and **victimising** of certain ethnic groups certainly wasn't news to Māori, who continue to suffer the effects of **colonisation, institutional racism** and **unconscious bias** to this day. They, too, saw alcohol used as a tool, first used to weaken them and then to keep them down. *'Alcohol sometimes greased the wheels of land sales, and was used to blunt the grief Māori communities experienced as a result of high rates of death and loss of land.'*

They, too, saw law enforcement and the justice system skewed against them — and still do. Although Māori made up only 15% of the population, in the 2013 census, Māori inmates made up 51% of sentenced prisoners in 2012 — and it's even higher in remand prisons (56%). In comparison, Pacific peoples made up only 7% of Aotearoa/New Zealand's population in 2013, yet 12% of prison inmates.

Unfortunately, this kind of imbalance is still seen in most indigenous populations and minority ethnic groups around the world. According to the United Nations, *'indigenous peoples frequently raise concerns about systemic discrimination and outright racism from the State and its authorities. This discrimination manifests itself in a number of ways such as frequent and unnecessary questioning by the police, condescending attitudes of teachers to students or rudeness from a receptionist in a government office. At their most extreme, these forms of discrimination lead to gross violations of human rights.'*

OUTING 'OVERSTAYERS'

It was this issue of 'overstaying' that led to the most overt racist attacks on people from Pacific nations at the time. Up until the early 1970s, the government had actively encouraged these people to come and solve the labour shortage, but by 1973 the economy was being squeezed by Britain's entry into the European Union, which reduced demand for exports, and a global 'oil shock', which sent the price of oil from US$3 per barrel to nearly $12 globally.[#88]

As the Aotearoa/New Zealand economy spiralled downwards, we saw the first real wave of unemployment experienced since the Great Depression of the 1930s. Rather than look at the underlying global causes of the recession, the arrival of so many people from Pacific nations was blamed, even though they had been actively encouraged to settle here during the economic boom. They made an easy target, already visible and already under attack. The jobs they had filled when no-one else wanted them were now being demanded back.

In 1974, Norman Kirk's Labour government clamped down on people overstaying the time allowed by their visas, despite the Immigration Department turning a blind eye when jobs were plentiful and their labour was needed. Although those from Pacific nations attracted the most attention, with Samoans and Tongans particularly affected,[#89] statistics show that through the 1970s and 1980s the majority of visa 'overstayers' actually came from Europe and North America. *'But they weren't targeted to anything like the same extent. Basically you had something like two-thirds of the overstayers were Europeans, but two-thirds of those prosecuted were Pacific Islanders.'* [#90] Racism meant the non-white overstayers were targeted.

'Suddenly these people who were welcomed when it suited New Zealand found themselves unwelcome when it didn't suit New Zealand.' Anthony "Aussie" Malcolm, NZ Immigration Minister 1981-1984 [#91]

POLITICAL FOOTBALLS

As this economic **recession** started to bite harder, migrants from the Pacific found their rights, including the right to reside here, kicked around like 'political footballs'[#92] — blamed by politicians and many Pākehā for more and more of the country's ills. The use of racist language also accelerated, as reported by W. G. Copwell, who wrote in a *Pacific Island Monthly* article: '*it comes as a shock to hear a friend, headmaster of a large primary school, refer to the Polynesian pupils under his control as 'Coconuts', and to be everywhere assaulted with the use of racist names such as 'head-hunter', 'tarpot', 'spear-thrower', 'wog', and 'wop'.*'[#93]

Can you imagine being on the receiving end of such racist taunts? Shamefully, some of you may still be subjected to them (or similar) today. For all that we can recite the old adage '*sticks and stones will break my bones but names will never hurt me*', the truth can be very different. As a post on the website of the Australian Human Rights Commission says:
'*In many cases people do not recognise their words and deeds are racist . . . I don't see that casual racism, via ignorant commentary or jokes, is acceptable. People who perceive they have the right and luxury to engage in racist practices do not understand that they are adding to a lifetime of injury for those of us who have had to navigate racism.*'[#94]

It has also been suggested that, given Māori had been burdened with racist stereotypes from the start of colonisation in Aotearoa/New Zealand , this 'lumping together' extended to the lumping of Māori and Pacific Island people together, with new Pacific migrants inheriting many of the negative **stereotypes** Pākehā had already inflicted on Māori.[#95] This claim is backed up by police attitudes when, during the crack-down on overstaying migrants, police would randomly stop anyone with 'brown' skin to question their immigration status, including Māori and other Aotearoa/New Zealand citizens from Niue, Tokelau, and the Cook Islands.[#96]

In 1973, Prime Minister Norman Kirk created a special police task force in Auckland to fight central city crime and 'deal' with overstayers. As the result of an amendment in 1968 to the 1964 Immigration Act (itself an update of the 1920 Act),[#97] this task force had powers to conduct random checks on any suspected overstayers — powers that allowed police to stop anyone on the street and demand proof of their visa status, and to go into homes and workplaces to carry out checks. So began the notion of 'dawn raids' — where police would arrive in the early hours of the morning, often with tracking dogs, to catch people in their beds so they had no chance to hide. Migrants were warned they should have their passports and immigration documents with them at all times.

For some, such actions reeked of South Africa's 'Pass Laws',[#98] especially as it became increasingly obvious that these random checks and 'dawn raids' focused solely on Pacific Island people. Human rights groups, along with some sections of the public and the media, began to question the fairness of such acts.[#99]

THE 2,000 STRONG MARCH AGAINST RACISM, WELLINGTON, OCTOBER 2004.

Eventually so much pressure was put on the Immigration Minister, Fraser Colman, that he suspended the raids until (he said) the government could develop a 'concerted plan.'[100] In a move designed to calm the criticism, Norman Kirk introduced a two–month 'partial **amnesty**' period in April 1974. During this time, overstayers were required to register themselves with Immigration in order to be granted a two–month visa extension.[101]

However, this change in policy was loudly criticised by the mainstream media, who continued to highlight any crimes or violence perpetrated by Māori and other Polynesians.[102] Although around 3,500 Tongans signed the overstayer register by the deadline, only 300 spaces were made available for 'well-settled' Tongans to be granted permanent residency.[103] When Auckland manufacturers argued that the deportations would damage factory production, the Government allowed businesses to identify and name 'key workers' who could stay. In all, 2,100 Tongans were nominated to stay a further two months, which stretched to eight months due to transportation issues.[104] There is no record of how many people who were instructed to leave actually left.

'CONSEQUENCES' CONFUSED WITH 'CAUSES'

One of the recurring accusations that would be used against Pacific Island communities at this time was the claim that they were the major contributors to crime. Carefully hand-picked crime statistics seemed to bear this out, with the major problems being identified as the abuse of alcohol, street disorder and violence.[105]

However, former police officer Luther Toloa, in the documentary *Dawn Raids*,[106] explained how the huge differences in lifestyle between Auckland and small, closely-knit villages (under strict Church control) back in the Islands led to such problems. All of a sudden, new migrants found themselves with extra money in their pockets that wasn't promised to the Church or family, so could be used to buy alcohol in the big central-city bars — described by Toloa as '*booze barns*.'[107] It didn't help that, outside of work and church, these bars were the only place to mingle with others from the Islands. Displaced from their own culture, and unwelcome in their new home, over-indulgence in alcohol was a way of numbing the difficulties and forgetting the stresses. However, as Toloa explained: '*for some that didn't work out well,*' especially for those not used to such free access to alcohol.[108]

Prime Minister Norman Kirk's task force was promoted as a response to 'drink-fuelled crime in the inner city.' The police would target the places where groups of Pacific people gathered and would arrest them for any minor offence. Many who swore or were drunk in public, or urinated in the street, were arrested, hugely inflating crime statistics. As Reverend Mua Strickson-Pua says: '*The police had a very bad reputation. They were considered racist. They were considered . . . not the friends of migrants, and yet I would well imagine that for certain white people, Pākehā people, they would have seen them as protectors of their rights. Our people saw them as the thugs, the thuggery, the gang part of the machinery of racism. And so, at that time, there wasn't a good relationship with the police in our communities.*'[109]

A Polynesian ex-police officer endorses this statement: '*I do believe that there was a very bigoted attitude from some of my colleagues at the time, for very minor offences which I really believe they could have just been given a warning for and sent home.*' [110]

NATIONAL PARTY 1975 ELECTION TV ADVERTISMENT

During the 1975 election campaign, a National Party TV advertisement played into Pākehā fears about excess migration, particularly stirring up negative racial feelings against Polynesian migrants. The cartoon, produced by an American animation studio, (excerpts shown here [111]) gives us a unique insight into mainstream racism at the time. Happy 'white' families stroll through parks, before a mass of aeroplanes bring in foreign workers. Obviously-Polynesian characters are blamed for job losses and violence, ruining life for the nice 'white' families. Images of 'brown' fists beating down on 'white' heads fuelled the racism of the message even more.

1: 'There was a time when New Zealand cities were quiet and clean . . . People said they were nice places to bring up children. . .'

2: '. . .but the cities grew alarmingly. People poured in, not just from the country but from other countries as well . . .'

3: ' . . . then one day there weren't enough jobs either . . . '

4: 'The people became angry and violence broke out, especially among those who had come from other places expecting great things . . .'

5: 'New Zealand cities aren't such nice places to bring up children any more . . .'

As a result of this concentrated policing and criminalising of those from Pacific nations, stereotyping them as thugs, drunken gangs, not as advanced as Pākehā New Zealanders, was commonplace. This stereotyping was reflected in the comments of a High Court judge who, in sentencing a Tongan man, said: *'one must have the gravest anxiety as to the placement of these unsophisticated people in an environment which many of them are totally unfitted to cope with.'* Robert Muldoon, National Party leader at the time, later cited this judge, saying his words proved the blame lay at the feet of *'unsophisticated Pacific Islanders being exposed to a pocketful of money and the wide open tavern door.'* [112]

Instead of viewing the behaviour that sprang from this disconnection to culture and community as a *consequence* of isolation, victimisation, poverty and bad policy, and working to fix the underlying causes, authorities chose to use such breaches of the peace as 'evidence' against Pacific Island people, in order to justify police acts.

ELECTION TIME: DOG-WHISTLE POLITICS

In the lead-up to the 1975 general election, the opposition National Party leader, Robert Muldoon, built his campaign around the racism being spread through newspapers and talkback radio.[113] He promised to reduce immigration and 'get tough' on law and order issues if elected, and blamed the Labour government's immigration policies for creating the economic recession and housing shortages.[114]

It is worth noting how often immigration still comes up as an election issue even today, with migrants of Asian descent, or of faiths other than Christian, now most often under the spotlight.

The 1975 National Party election advertisement (see Pg 69), in addition to its overt racism, was an example of what is now known as *'dog-whistle politics'*, taken from the idea that a dog-whistle can only be heard by dogs. In politics, it refers to a coded message transmitted through words or phrases commonly understood by a particular group of people, but not by others. In the case of this advertisement, the pictures worked as the silent whistle to give the words added racist meaning to those already inclined to think this way. This also gave media the go-ahead to target Pacific Island migrants, with headlines such as *'Brown's out – White's all right', 'Kiwis must come first',* and *'Send all the illegals back home'* [115] appearing on articles blaming Pacific Island migrants for all crimes, and rape most particularly. This strategy clearly worked, with the National Party winning the election with the biggest majority ever seen in Aotearoa/New Zealand.

THE REINTRODUCTION OF RAIDS AT DAWN

With Robert Muldoon's election in 1975, he now had the power to step-up harassment of the Pacific Island community. A designated 'enemy' is a potent political assett. He instructed police and Immigration officials to join forces and begin a concerted crackdown on 'overstayers'.

'Anyone who speaks in a non-Kiwi accent or looks as though he was not born in this country should carry a passport.'
Auckland Police Chief Superintendent Berriman quoted in the Auckland Star newspaper 22.10.76

The Immigration Department were ordered to draw up arrest warrants, and the police were tasked with making the arrests. In defence of these actions, the newly-appointed Immigration Minister, Frank Gill, was quoted as saying: *'We can't let a flood come here and swamp us and swamp our economy.'*[116] Police Minister, Allan McCready (an ex-dairy farmer), replied when asked how police would know if someone was an overstayer, *'Well, I can tell a Jersey [cow] from a Friesian.'* #117

Raids on houses and workplaces began again, with much more frequency and ruthlessness. With many Polynesian workers leaving at 5am or 6am for work, police would arrive in the early hours of the morning and cover all windows and exits before knocking on the door, often with police dogs straining on their leads. The following quotes are taken from the documentary 'Dawn Raids', directed by Damon Fepulea'I, Isola Productions, 2005:

'I was startled to wake and find that police had surrounded the house. I tried jumping outside . . . but there was another policeman at the door. So I thought I'd hide in the wardrobe, however the dog sniffed me out.'

'My cousin confronted them for a search warrant and tried to chase them out. However the police were determined to take us all at that time. So we were taken away with nothing but the clothes on our backs to jail and placed in cells.'

'I was taken by surprise, when these men came and took me from work. They said I would be questioned and then returned . . . [but] that was the last time I saw anyone, including my family.' #118

'OPERATION POT BLACK', 20 OCTOBER 1976

Police launched 'Operation Pot Black', another intensive campaign of random checks, stopping anyone with 'brown' skin, demanding proof of residency. In their eagerness to flush out overstayers, they often stopped Māori and other Pacific Island people who were legally allowed to stay here. In four days from the Thursday to Sunday, police stopped and questioned more than 800 Polynesians about their immigration status, many at random. On 26 October, the *Auckland Star* published the statement of a woman of Tuhoe descent stopped by police.

'I was going to work last Friday morning. We got off the bus at Rawene Road, Highbury about 7:30. There was myself, a Samoan girl, a European and two Fijians. A police car stopped across the road from us. One called 'can we see you?' They asked me and the Samoan girl which island we were from. The Samoan girl said Western Samoa. I realised what it was all about and I said 'I'm a Māori.' The policeman said 'hope you're a good Maori.' There were two men cops and a lady. They were sniggering through it. They didn't ask me anything else after that. He then questioned the Samoan girl, who luckily had her papers. The Fijians look like Maoris and weren't questioned. They didn't know any of our names and didn't ask questions about anything else.'
Reported in Auckland Star, 26.10.76 #119

A young Tongan man, who was legally living in Aotearoa/New Zealand , was stopped three times:

'On Thursday night I was drinking in the Rising Sun Hotel. At 9:30 I left the pub and walked along Karangahape Road towards Ponsonby. A police car stopped and a policeman stopped me and asked me which island I came from, how long I had been here, and where my passport was. I showed him my letter from the Labour Department ... and he let me go. He did not know my name, he did not ask me anything else. I continued to the Star Hotel for a drink. A policeman inside stopped me and asked the same questions. I left and started walking home about 10 o'clock. Along Great North Road, a police car pulled up close to the Labour Department. A policeman got out and asked me the same questions. I showed them the form and they left. Then I went home.'
Reported in the Auckland Star 27.10.76

Pua Sofi, Chairman of the Samoan Advisory Council at the time, described seeing four policemen on one side of the road and six on the other, stopping anyone with 'brown' skin from passing. *'The only people they were letting through were Europeans.'* [120] As if to confirm this, Chief Superintendent Berriman told media that police would stop and question *'anyone who does not look like a New Zealander, or who speaks with a foreign accent. . . These people must expect to arouse suspicion',* despite the fact that by the time he said this there were 60,000 legal permanent residents from various Pacific Islands. [121]

HANG ON A MOMENT! DIDN'T ANYONE STAND UP FOR THEM?

Yes, indeed.

The Dawn Raids raids caused plenty of public outcry. The Tongan community, the Federation of Labour (FOL), the Citizens Association for Racial Equality (CARE), who were also very active during the 1981 anti-Springbok Tour campaign, the Polynesian Panther Party (see pages 76-77), the Race Relations Council, and Ngā Tamatoa all expressed concern at the very narrow targeting of one multi-cultural ethnic group. [122]

In essence, these groups all argued that employers had encouraged workers to come, most were well settled, and therefore they should be given a general amnesty. They also criticised the police's heavy-handed tactics, including wrongful arrests and people being arrested in their pyjamas and having to later appear in court still wearing them or in borrowed clothing.

'It is as if these people have committed some ghastly crime, a murder or a rape. Does any person deserve to be hurried away in the middle of the night because he has overstayed his permit?' [123]
Tongan community spokesperson.

Clive Edwards, a prominent Tongan lawyer, claimed that the Government's attitude to Pacific Island immigrants made racial prejudice *'a respectable thing.'* [124] During the raids in Norman Kirk's time as Prime Minister, CARE had also attempted to prevent 40 overstayers from being deported back to

POSTER PRODUCED FOR AMNESTY AROHA (ORGANISATION), 1976.

Tonga on the British cruise ship *Ocean Monarch*, by convincing the crew to refuse to sail if the Tongans were loaded aboard. To prevent public confrontation at the wharf, the deportees where instead flown out in secret the next day. The Borough Council of Onehunga also protested and called for amnesty for overstayers, and the Tongan Society, along with the Tongan Church, organised a 3,000 signature petition, also calling for amnesty.[125]

By this time, the media were growing more critical of the raids and the *Christchurch Star* accused police and Immigration of using 'gestapo tactics.' As public and media outcry intensified, an official report into how the issue was being handled was commissioned and it eventually concluded that '*police procedures in pursuing illegal immigrants were a mess.*'[126] It laid the bulk of the blame on the Immigration Division, rather than the politics involved, or the racism.

By the Tuesday after 'Operation Pot Black', the Labour opposition also began an attack on the Government's actions. There were calls for the Ministers of Police and Immigration to step down, and Labour's MP for Onehunga, Franks Rogers, described the raids as '*sickening and sad*', and said that '*Hitler used these tactics and so did Mussolini.*'[127] Many in the anti-racist movement and other civil liberty groups began to voice concerns, even National MPs. The Pacific Island Advisory Council declared that the raids '*confirmed more than ever our suspicion that your Government is setting out to legalise racial prejudice*' and the Samoan Advisory Council added: '*the indiscriminate questioning of Islanders in the street by police is outrageous because it highlights the hypocrisy of this so-called harmonious and multicultural society.*'[129]

The tide was turning.

More and more questions were being asked in Parliament. More and more groups started speaking out against the checks and raids, including the Auckland Trades Council, the Māori Women's Welfare League, the Auckland Tongan Society, the United Nations Association, the Presbyterian Church, the Pacific Islands Council, the Auckland District Māori Council, the Pacific Islands Housing and Welfare Association, CARE, the Auckland Committee on Racism and Discrimination, the Inter-Church Trade and Industry Mission, the Samoan Action Organisation, the Public Service Association, the Federation of University Women, the Post Primary Teachers Association, the Methodist Church, and twenty Anglican churchmen, including the Bishop and the Dean of Auckland. In Wellington many of these groups came together and formed Amnesty Aroha.[130]

In Auckland the Polynesian Panthers were planning a little dawn raiding of their own.

WE ARE THE POLYNESIAN PANTHERS . . . HEAR US ROAR!

On 16 June, 1971, a group of young people, mainly between 17 and 19 years of age, came together in Auckland, inspired by the US Black-empowerment movement, the Black Panthers. This mixed group of young Pasifika people — many of them born in Aotearoa/New Zealand — joined forces to challenge the racist attitudes they saw all around them, for the good of all Aotearoa/New Zealand . Founded by young men — particularly Fred Schmidt, Nooroa Teavae, Paul Dapp, Vaughan Sanft, Eddie Williams, Ta Iuli and Will 'Ilolahia[131]— the Polynesian Panther movement wanted to depict the true essence of Pacific people and their culture, and to undo the damage caused by the anti-Islander campaigns they saw all around them. They also desired the empowerment of their people, and to show others how to stand up to unjust laws and treatment through the power of peaceful protest.[132]

Eventually other chapters were also started in South Auckland, Christchurch, Dunedin, several prisons, and in Sydney.

Their motto was '*Educate to liberate*' and they attracted around 500 members [133] to their movement, which stated as its goals:
- To show that Polynesian children should make use of the education system available and become capable citizens;
- To promote Polynesian culture among both Pacific Island peoples and Europeans in order to obtain better understanding;
- To prevent racism, of all forms, in Aotearoa/ New Zealand;
- Encouragement of awareness of each other's cultures;
- Decent housing fit for human occupation.

Alongside the goals sat several rules:
- No use or possession of drugs or alcohol;
- no possession of weapons or any other harmful device;
- no using the name of the movement in public for self-glory;
- equality of the sexes.

They appointed a chairman and secretary and various ministries, including defence, information (to challenge racists stereotypes), culture and Panther youth. Their leader, Will 'Ilolahia, a former member of a gang of youths called the Nigs, fought hard to shake off the 'gang' label and, instead, established the Polynesian Panthers as a credible force for good, stressing non-violent action. [135]

'We had to spend a lot of our early time period trying to dispel the gang myth, so we ended up doing programmes like taking elderly folks on bus trips and delivering community newspapers . . . just to kill the image that we were a gang.' Will 'Ilolahia. [136]

Few women joined, as membership was made difficult by strict culturally-defined roles. Those who overcame the obstacles include Melani Anae, Miriama Rauhihi, Etta Gillon, and Vicki Mae. Dr. Melani Anae went on to become a respected and powerful voice in academia, authoring a chapter in the 2012 Te Papa Press book *Tangata O Le Moana* which looks specifically at the dawn raids, overstayers and the Polynesian Panthers, well worth reading.

These women provided a good balance to the all-male leadership, though often ended up dispatched to the kitchen, catering for meetings and events. It seems that cultural behaviours endure even during a political transformation such as this.

Using skills learnt through supporting Māori at the Bastion Point occupation [137] and Waitangi Day protests,[138] they joined forces with many local groups — including the Tenants Aid Brigade, churches and community workers, and anti-racist groups such as Ngā Tamatoa, HART, CARE, ACORD and the Ponsonby People's Union —and roped

POLYNESIAN PANTHERS MEMBERS PROTEST THE DAWN RAID POLICY

in others to set up better social supports for the Polynesian community. They organised and manned after-school homework centres with the help of CARE and local high-school teachers, started petitions, lobbied for traffic lights on dangerous intersections, fought racist and negligent landlords, ran food programmes, organised prison visits so families could see their loved-ones, and supported those caught up in the random checks and dawn raids. #139

With the help of lawyer David Lange (later Prime Minister of Aotearoa/New Zealand from 1984 to 1989), they produced Aotearoa/New Zealand's first **legal aid booklet**, which spelt out people's civil rights if they were stopped or arrested, and distributed these throughout the community.

As random police checks and raids grew worse, they set up the Police Investigation Group (PIG), and (along with groups such as CARE and the People's Union) began following the paddy wagons as the police went about their checks, ready to record any wrong-doing or to assist the people who were stopped. They also followed police into the bars and pubs, taking photographs as evidence and distributing their information booklets. #140

Despite the good they were doing, many older community members and family were very uncomfortable with their actions, used to obeying rules and reluctant to make a fuss. Some within the Pacific community even reported others to the police as overstayers, not liking how the controversy was 'ruining it for everyone.' #141 But the Panthers persisted, eventually winning many over with their pro-community activities.

'In the Panther days we had a lot of non-support from our parents because they were very appreciative that they were able to come to Aotearoa and get work. And because of the traditional Polynesian humbleness, they questioned our right to stand up and protest. And we explained to them that we had a right because we were New Zealand-born.'
Will 'Ilolahia, speaking to Dale Husband in E-tangata Sun 22 May 2016 #142

By 1976, the Polynesian Panthers came up with a powerful new strategy at a time when politicians were still loudly denying the brutal facts of the checks and raids. The Panthers began 'dawn raids' of politicians' houses by banging on the door, spotlights blazing, demanding to see passports, and running away as politicians came to the door.[143]

Tigilau Ness, one of the original Panthers and a legendary musician, recalled the night the Panthers went to the home of Bill Birch, one of National's Government Ministers. *'We were calling out on loudhailers at three o'clock in the morning: Bill Birch, come out with your passport now!'* [144]

Another time, they surrounded the house of Minister George Gair and turned their spotlights on. Through loud hailers they yelled for Gair to come out and show his passport. As soon as the house lights came on they jumped in their cars and left. The next day George Gair responded to a question about the 'raid' from Radio Hauraki: *'How dare these people come at such an ungodly hour?'* A radio announcer retorted: *'Well, surely that's what they're complaining about?'* [145] The Panther's point was made and two and a half weeks later, the Government finally backed down and the raids were stopped. The Polynesian Panthers would go on to support Māori activists Ngā Tamatoa and others in championing Māori rights and the anti-Springbok Tour campaign [146] Today they continue to inspire new Pacific generations.

'The members of the Panthers have gone on to good things: teachers, lecturers, ministers . . . We haven't all been killed off as revolutionaries. Our main aim was then, and still is now, equality and a more peaceable Aotearoa. So until that happens, we will always be going.' Tigilau Ness. [147]

WHAT DOES ALL THIS MEAN FOR AOTEAROA TODAY?

Despite courageous and collective community action bringing the 1970s dawn raids to an end, that particular hostile racism towards Pacific peoples continued into the 1980s. In 1986, 86% of those prosecuted for overstaying were still people from Pacific nations, although only a third of all overstayers were from there. As in the past, the majority of overstayers were white, and from Europe and North America. Poor working conditions, sub-standard accommodation and living standards, and unequal pay were, and continue to be, very real.

However, the main challenge for Pacific people remains: how they are perceived. The damage done by the outpouring of racist talk and blame is hard to shift, and many groups were and are kept busy trying to challenge this.

By the 1990s public attitudes were finally changing, with the majority of Pacifika peoples by then Aotearoa/New Zealand -born. In 2013, 62.3 % of people (181,791 people) who identified with at least one Pacific ethnicity were born in Aotearoa/New Zealand. In comparison, the proportion of Aotearoa/New Zealand -born Pacific peoples in previous censuses was 60.0 % (157,203 people) in 2006, and 58.2 % (133,791 people) in 2001.[148] Thanks to the education and empowerment made possible by groups such as the Polynesian Panthers, and the heightened awareness of racism that sprang from the 1981 Springbok Tour, people of Pacific Island descent began to be recognised as having a positive impact on public life. In the early 21st century, with over a quarter of a million people of Pacific ethnicity in Aotearoa/New Zealand, levels of public intolerance lessened. In 2014 a record number of MPs identified as Pacific peoples, comprising 7% of the Parliament, up from 5% in 2011. [149] The 2017 general election saw the number drop back slightly to 6.7%, though the combined total of Māori and other Pacific peoples was 29%.[#150] Current Members of Parliament with ties to the Pacific include: Carmel Sepuloni, Jenny Salesa, Kris Fa'afoi, and Aupito William Sio. Bernadette Pereira, the head of Pacific women's group Pacifica Inc, said it was wonderful for the local Pacific community. '*It is a proud moment for the Pacific communities around New Zealand to have good Pacific representation in Parliament at ministerial level.*'[#151]

A survey in 2009 found that 58% of respondents believed there was some discrimination against Pacific peoples, but only 5% of respondents believed they were now the group most discriminated against.[#152] Yet, for many of those Pacific peoples, along with Māori, still struggling at the bottom of income and social measures, we can do much better.

For instance, in April of 2018, media brought to light a new pilot Immigration New Zealand crack-down on overstayers which appeared to once again target people from Pacific nations through 'ethnic profiling.' Melino Maka from the Tongan Advisory Council described it as racist and said he feared Pasifika people could be unfairly targeted. '*This is bringing back the dawn raids. You can see the language they use, "using up our health system" — that's the same language they use in America and Europe to justify using some of those racist policies that we don't need here in New Zealand.*'[#153]

It is encouraging to note that when challenged on this, the new Immigration Minister, Iain Lees-Galloway, called for the pilot to be put on 'hold' so it could be properly assessed.[#154]

DOES THIS MEAN THE LESSONS OF OUR RACIST PAST ARE FINALLY BEING LEARNT?

It would be nice to think so. Certainly, the influence of Pacific Island culture is now a part of mainstream Aotearoa/New Zealand, thanks to the ground-breaking efforts of many who brought Pasifika into popular culture through plays, films, comedy, novels, poetry, dance, cartoons, acting, visual arts and, of course, the magnificent Polyfest, the largest Polynesian Festival in the world.[#155]

Unfortunately, in many ways, the racism and hostility towards Pacific island migrants has now been replaced by a similar resentment to Asian migrants, particularly those from China. Despite the fact that it is now recognised that connection to one's culture and heritage is one of the most positive and necessary requirements for human well-being, the age-old racist arguments and rhetoric have again been raised. As the Auckland house-market is squeezed tighter and tighter in 2018, and houses have become increasingly unaffordable to many, scape-goats are again being blamed — and the same old arguments against immigrants are being wheeled out.

'New Zealand loved telling the world, for twenty years straight after the war, that we were the most multi-cultural society, that we were the best at treating coloured people, and that we had a relationship. It didn't. It was still only in the beginning of really becoming a nation that understood what it meant to deal with all peoples that were coming to this nation.' Reverend Mua Strickson-Pua.[#156]

In a world where political unrest and climate change will see more and more people forced to leave the place of their birth to find new homes in other countries with work and other opportunities, our attitudes to migrants and refugees really needs an overhaul — and a good injection of empathy and compassion. Any person, anywhere, can suddenly find themselves displaced or making the brave decision to uproot themselves for the betterment and safety of their families. If we acted on the basis that it could happen to us, and thought about how *we* would like to welcomed and supported if the need arose, then maybe we can rid ourselves of this 'them' and 'us' racist mentality, and truly make Aotearoa New Zealand the multi-cultural paradise people have claimed it to be for so long.

CHRIS SLADE: THE UN-LEVEL PLAYING FIELD

THIS CARTOON EXPLORES THE 'UN-LEVEL PLAYING FIELD' IN TERMS OF EDUCATION BUT IT COULD EQUALLY APPLY TO MANY OTHER EXAMPLES OF STRUCTURAL OR INVISIBLE PRIVILEGE. IT ACKNOWLEDGES THAT NOT EVERYONE STARTS FROM THE SAME LEVEL OF ADVANTAGE.

SHARON MURDOCH: ON TOLERANCE AND ACCEPTANCE & LET'S UNRAVEL IT

1945-1960s: Aotearoa/New Zealand's economy grows and workers from Pacific nations are recruited by the NZ government to fill job vacancies, particularly in low-skilled and factory jobs.

1961-1971: Pacific island migrants rise from 12,000 people to 48,000. An estimated 20,000 people from Pacific nations are settled in Auckland by 1968.

1968: An amendment to the Immigration Act is passed, allowing deportation of anyone overstaying their work permits. Police were given powers to demand passports and paperwork and to arrest anyone who did not obey immediately. This gave a green-light to random checks and dawn raids.

1971: On June 16th the Polynesian Panther Movement is founded.

TIMELINE

1973: The NZ economy is squeezed by Britain's entry to the EU and a global 'oil shock.' Unemployment rises sharply. Prime Minister Norman Kirk creates a special police task force in Auckland to 'deal' with overstayers and inner city crime.

1974: NZ Police conduct more 'dawn raids' on suspected overstayers, focusing predominantly on Polynesians. In response to criticism, the Immigration Minister, Fraser Colman, suspends the raids until the government develops a 'concerted plan.'

April: Norman Kirk introduces a two-month amnesty, with registered overstayers granted a two-month visa extension.

July: National Party leader, Robert Muldoon, promises to reduce immigration and 'get tough' on law and order issues if elected. He blames the Labour government's immigration policies for worsening the economic recession and housing shortages.

1975: The National Party's anti-migrant electoral advertisements lead them to win with the largest majority in NZ history. The Immigration Department issues warrants for overstayers and police action them, many at during the night or at dawn.

1976: Immigration Minister Frank Gill announces a 12-week halt of the raids, requiring people to register as overstayers to avoid arrest. By July 5th, 4,647 overstayers have registered, all but 70 from Pacific Island nations. 'Operation Pot Black' is launched on the 20th of October. Over four days, more than 800 Polynesians are stopped and questioned. The Polynesian Panthers begin 'dawn raids' on Government Ministers. Eventually the raids and random checks are halted, after much public outcry.

SHIPS, SPIES & SABOTAGE

THE BOMBING OF THE RAINBOW WARRIOR

In early July, 1985, the Greenpeace ship *Rainbow Warrior* **sailed triumphantly into Auckland harbour after helping over 300 members**[157] **of the Rongelap community relocate away from their home island in the Marshall Islands (North Pacific), to escape contamination from the US nuclear testing that took place thirty-one years before.** [158]

The ship was met in the harbour by a fleet of small boats, all excited to see the newly refitted ship and welcome her to our shores. As the Rainbow Warrior moored at Marsden Dock, well-wishers crowded around to greet them and hear the crews' plans to lead a *flotilla* of local boats to the small atoll of Mururoa, in French Polynesia, to protest against the French nuclear testing taking place there.

Three days later, on the 10th July, as midnight drew near, most of the crew were tucked up in their bunks, while a few stragglers huddled around the table, chatting as they shared the last two bottles of beer left over from a crew member's birthday celebration.

Little did they know that three hours earlier, two stealthy **saboteurs** had sped across the harbour in an inflatable dingy before diving under the hull of the Rainbow Warrior. There they attached a 10 kg **limpet mine** to the propeller shaft and a larger mine to the

> **KEYWORDS**
>
> **Activist** - an especially active, vigorous supporter of a cause, especially a political cause.
>
> **Boycott** - withdraw from commercial or social relations with (a country, organization, or person) as a punishment or protest.
>
> **Compensation** - something, typically money, awarded to someone in recognition of loss, suffering, or injury.
>
> **Contamination** - the act of making something impure or unsuitable by contact with something unclean, bad, etc. In the case of nuclear weapons, this means radioactive fallout.
>
> **Flotilla** – a group all moving together, usually at sea.
>
> **Ground zero** - where an activity begins or occurs
>
> **Limpet mine** - A mine (bomb) designed to be attached magnetically to a ship's hull and set to explode after a certain time.
>
> **Proliferation** - a rapid and often excessive spread or increase, for example nuclear proliferation.
>
> **Radioactive fallout** - the settling of radioactive airborne particles ejected into the atmosphere from nuclear explosions onto the ground, water and people.
>
> **Relocate** - to move (a building, population, etc.) to a different location.
>
> **Saboteur** - a person who commits or practices sabotage (underhand and/or illegal interference).
>
> **Scuttled** - to cut a hole through the bottom, deck, or side of a ship specifically to sink it.
>
> **Sovereignty** - a sovereign or independent state, community, or political unit.
>
> **Unparalleled** - having no parallel or equal; exceptional.

hull right next to the engine room, both timed to go off 11.50pm that night. Bombs set, they fled back to their hidden Zodiac and vanished into the darkness.

Right on cue, the first explosion tore open a huge hole into the engine room. The lights went out and the crack of breaking glass was followed by the roar of rushing water. The blast was so brutal it shunted a freighter on the other side of wharf a whole five metres sideways. The shocked crew leapt for dry land, thinking at first they'd been hit by another boat, as the captain, Peter Willcox, rushed towards the engine room.

There he found the chief engineer, Davey Edwards, shaking his head and saying, '*it's all over, she's finished.*' Willcox later said: '*The first mate was at the bottom of the stairs leading to the lower accommodation. I asked him if everyone was up and he said yes. That's when the second bomb went off, right under our feet . . .*' He ordered everyone to abandon the ship. '*I stood there looking at the boat with all the bubbles coming out of it. That's when Davey said Fernando is down there. I remember arguing with him, saying … Fernando has gone to town, that's what he always did. No he said. Fernando is [still] down there.*' [159]

The ship's Dutch/Portuguese photographer, Fernando Pereira, [160] who had waved goodbye to his wife, small son and daughter three months earlier, was eager to bring his photographs of the nuclear testing and the effects of previous **radioactive fallout** to the wider world.

Pereira was, indeed, still inside. He had raced down the narrow stairway, trying to rescue his cameras from one of the stern cabins. It was thought the second explosion left him stunned, and that he drowned when his camera straps snagged around his legs. He had just celebrated his 35th birthday.

As the shocked crew watched from the wharf, the Rainbow Warrior tipped towards the dock and sank, its keel digging into the harbour floor. All this took no more than four minutes. At first everyone supposed something had exploded on board the ship. But, as the morning dawned, police divers confirmed that the source of the explosion was external. Within hours, news organisations all around the world were reporting that this was no dreadful accident; this was an act of terrorism, intent on sabotage and murder.

FERNANDO AND HIS DAUGHTER

THE RAINBOW WARRIOR

First commissioned as a North Sea fisheries vessel in 1956, the ship was bought by Greenpeace in 1977 and christened the *Rainbow Warrior*. Volunteers resurrected the rusting ship, which was 49 metres long, with 22 berths (bunks). They repainted it and overhauled its engines before its first campaign against Iceland's commercial whaling fleet in June 1978. Later they would fit masts and sails, to make it more environmentally sustainable.

THE RAINBOW WARRIOR AFTER THE BOMBING

The unravelling of the mystery makes for fascinating reading. Through a combination of thorough police work and a general public just as eager to fill the gaps, the lead-up to the attack and its aftermath were pieced together like a giant jigsaw puzzle. Phil Taylor of the New Zealand Herald wrote an excellent overview of the puzzle pieces in this online feature:
http://features.nzherald.co.nz/rainbow-warrior/

Logo credit: "Trademark of Stichting Greenpeach Council"

GREENPEACE

WHO AND WHAT ARE GREENPEACE?

According to their website, Greenpeace is an independent global campaigning organisation that acts to change attitudes and behaviour, to protect and conserve the environment and to promote peace by

- Catalysing an energy revolution to address the number one threat facing our planet: climate change.
- Defending our oceans by challenging wasteful and destructive fishing, and creating a global network of marine reserves.
- Protecting the world's ancient forests and the animals, plants and people that depend on them.
- Protecting the world's ancient forests and the animals, plants and people that depend on them.
- Working for disarmament and peace by tackling the causes of conflict and calling for the elimination of all nuclear weapons.
- Creating a toxic free future with safer alternatives to hazardous chemicals in today's products and manufacturing.
- Campaigning for sustainable agriculture by rejecting genetically engineered organisms, protecting biodiversity and encouraging socially responsible farming.

Greenpeace is present in 40 countries across Europe, The Americas, Asia, Africa and the Pacific.

https://www.greenpeace.org/new-zealand/

THE BOMBING WAS WIDELY REPORTED INCLUDING THESE STORIES FROM THE NZ HERALD

WHAT HAPPENED NEXT?

As the country reeled in shock, questions snowballed. Who would do such a thing? And why would they do it? Slowly the police evidence mounted and the truth that unfolded read like something from a spy novel. Within three days of the blasts, Cabinet ministers in Aotearoa/New Zealand's parliament were told that the finger of blame pointed damningly in France's direction. Over the following days, information flooded in from the public, eager to solve the crime. By the tenth day after the sinking, enough evidence had been pieced together for the government to forward the police file to the New Zealand embassy in Paris, who delivered it to the headquarters of France's foreign ministry. The game was up. This evidence showed that a group of French agents from their foreign intelligence services had planned and carried out the raid. Named *Operation Satanic*, it was driven by the most high-ranking officials in the French government in an attempt to halt the Greenpeace protests against French nuclear testing in the Pacific.

This act of terrorism on behalf of the French government was an attack on our **sovereignty** and people's right to peaceful protest, designed to shut the issue down. But, instead, the outrage was so great that support for Greenpeace (until that time considered a 'fringe' group) increased enormously. The bombing led to an anti-nuclear movement that culminated in Aotearoa/New Zealand passing its ground-breaking anti-nuclear legislation in 1987.

'When we initially said we knew all about the [French] bombers, they just laughed. It was only when we produced the file that they realised just what detail we had of the agents' movements. They acknowledged their secret service had been in New Zealand. They started talking to us on more realistic terms.' Head of the Prime Minister's Department at the time, Gerald Hensley, speaking of the affair twenty years later.

91

THE BOMBING OF THE RAINBOW WARRIOR #161

The Rainbow Warrior bombing took place on July 10, 1985, but it had been in the planning stages for months, and had repercussions that would shape New Zealand's future.

1985

23 April: French agent Christine Huguette Cabon arrives in Auckland and starts volunteering for Greenpeace. She claims to be against the nuclear testing, befriending other activists and gaining access to Greenpeace plans and operations.

24 May: Christine Huguette Cabon departs New Zealand.

13 June: The French yacht 'Ouvea' departs Noumea, New Caledonia, for New Zealand. On board are French agents Roland Verge, Gerald Andries, Jean-Michel Bartelo and Xavier Maniguet. They have on board a Zodiac inflatable boat, outboard motor, diving equipment and explosives.

22 June: French yacht Ouvea arrives at Parengarenga Harbour, Northland. Agents Alain Mafart and Dominique Prieur arrive in Auckland from France and rent a campervan to meet with the 'Ouvea' crew.

23 June: French agent Louis Pierre Dillais arrives in Auckland.

7 July: The Rainbow Warrior arrives in Auckland. French agents Jean Cammas and Jean Luc Kister arrive in Auckland to carry out the bombing.

9 July: The French yacht 'Ouvea' departs Whangarei for Norfolk Island.

10 July: The Rainbow Warrior is sunk by two limpet mines. Fernando Pereira is killed.

11 July: French agents Dillais, Cammas and Klister cross Cook Strait to the South Island.

12 July: Mafart and Prieur are caught by police while returning their campervan. The French government denies involvement in the bombing.

15 July: NZ Police detectives interview three of the 'Ouvea' crew on Norfolk Island. They gather evidence but have to release them. The yacht later disappears on the voyage to Noumea and the crew turn up in France.

23 July: French agent Louis Pierre Dillais flies to Australia.

26 July: French agents Jean Cammas and Jean Luc Kister fly from Auckland to Tahiti.

4 August: Mafart and Prieur are charged with murder.

8 August: French Prime Minister Laurent Fabius announces an inquiry into who was responsible for the bombing. Bernard Tricot, a senior civil servant, is to lead the inquiry.

26 August: The French Tricot inquiry clears the French authorities of involvement in the bombing. The Tricot report states that the agents were only gathering intelligence about the upcoming anti-nuclear testing protests at Mururoa.

TIMELINE

17 September: The French Le Monde newspaper makes allegations of French involvement.

20 September: French Defence Minister Charles Hernu resigns and DGSE #162 head Pierre Lacoste is sacked over the scandal.

22 September: French Prime Minister Laurent Fabius makes a television broadcast stating that French agents of the DGSE sank the Rainbow Warrior. They were under orders and therefore would not be punished.

4 November: Mafart and Prieur plead guilty to the charge of manslaughter and wilful damage.

22 November: Mafart and Prieur are sentenced to 10 years' jail in New Zealand.

CHRISTINE CABON: READ HER STORY ON PG 105

1986
July: France pays New Zealand NZ$13m in **compensation**. Prieur and Mafart are sent to Hao Atoll in French Polynesia for three years to serve their sentence. Prieur's husband joins her there.

1987
2 October: France is ordered to pay Greenpeace more than US$8.1m in compensation.

12 December: The Rainbow Warrior is **scuttled** at Matauri Bay off Northland's coast.

14 December: Alain Mafart returns to France due to illness. He is later decorated and promoted.

1988
6 May: Dominique Prieur returns to France early due to pregnancy. She is later decorated and promoted.

TIMELINE REPRODUCED WITH THANKS TO GREENPEACE.

THE CONTEXT: HOW ON EARTH DID IT COME TO THIS?

"Might not a bomb no bigger than an orange be found to possess a secret power to destroy a whole block of buildings—nay to concentrate the force of a thousand tons of cordite and blast a township at a stroke?" Winston Churchill, 1924.

To properly unravel this astounding chapter of our history, we need to travel back in time. In a strange twist, this whole nuclear story started with Aotearoa/New Zealander Ernest Rutherford, who first split the atom in 1917, claiming he had *'broken the machine and touched the ghost of matter.'*[163] Nuclear fission, which opened up the possibilities of producing nuclear power and weapons, was discovered two years after his death in 1937.

During World War II, the United States, UK and Canada collaborated in the **Manhattan Project**, racing to harness nuclear fission as a weapon before a suspected Nazi German atomic bomb project could succeed. In August 1945, two fission bombs were dropped on Japan — the first on the city of Hiroshima on August the 6th, and then a second on the city of Nagasaki on the 9th. Such was the **unparalleled** level of death and destruction, Japan agreed to an unconditional surrender on August 14, 1945, finally bringing World War II to an end.

But while our allies rejoiced that the war was over, on the ground at Hiroshima and Nagasaki, the horror was unlike anything seen before. In Hiroshima, the bomb killed or wounded nearly 130,000 people, with intense fires gutting everything within a 2 kilometre radius. Of the 286,00 people living in Nagasaki at the time of the blast, an estimated 74,000 were killed and another 75,000 sustained severe injuries,[164] with more people dying from the effects in the following months. Moreover, the effects of the radioactive fallout would continue to affect those who survived for many decades after the initial blast and even impacted on future generations.

ABOVE: HIROSHIMA

RIGHT: THE HIROSHIMA GENBAKU DOME AFTER THE BOMBING.

THE YEARS THAT FOLLOWED WERE NOT EASY FOR SURVIVORS. THEY BECAME KNOWN AS THE HIBAKUSHA — THE "BOMB-AFFECTED PEOPLE". THERE WERE MORE THAN 400,000, THOSE WHO SURVIVED HIROSHIMA AND NAGASAKI. IMAGE TAKEN FROM: HTTP://HIROSHIMA.AUSTRALIANDOCTOR.COM.AU

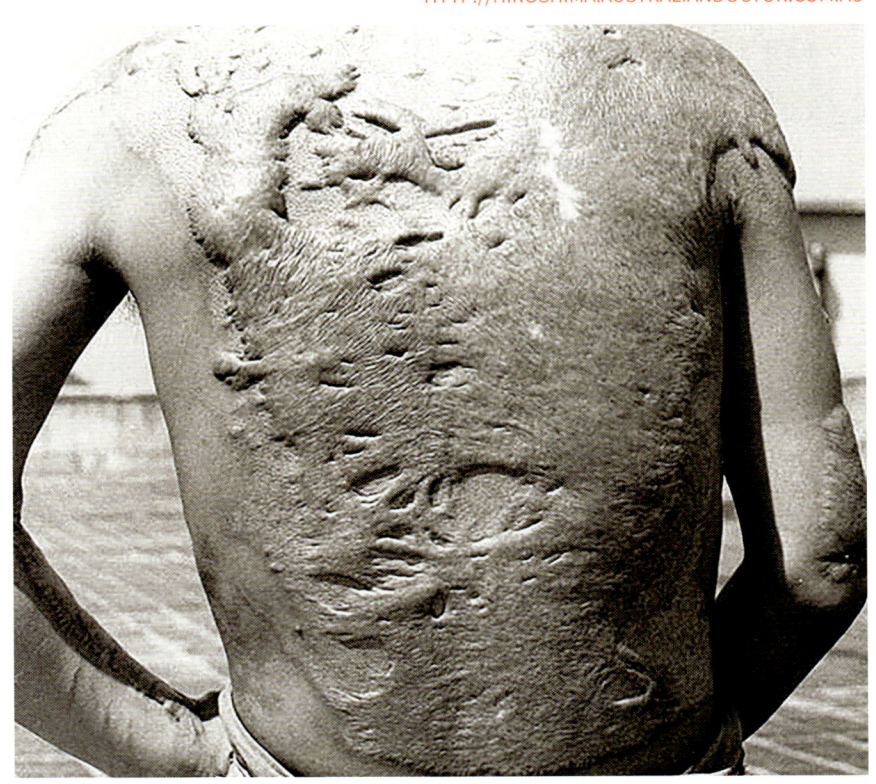

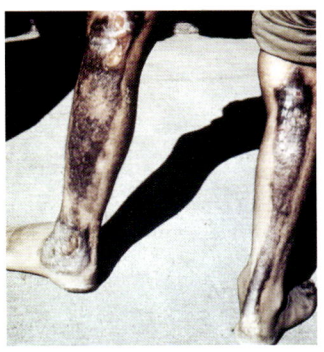

ABOVE: DIRECT, THERMAL NUCLEAR FLASH BURNS

RIGHT: HIROSHIMA RESIDENTS AFTER THE BOMBING

The use of this technology left the world forever changed. The nuclear monster had been uncaged.

In the years immediately following the end of the war, the US, the Soviet Union and Great Britain all carried out nuclear weapons tests, until India's president, Jawaharlal Nehru, called for a ban on nuclear testing in 1954.[#164] This was to be the first major attempt to outlaw using nuclear technology for weapons of mass destruction, and was followed by nearly 10,000 scientists presenting a petition to the United Nations Secretary-General in 1958 that pleaded:

'We deem it imperative that immediate action be taken to effect an international agreement to stop testing of all nuclear weapons.'[#164]

For an excellent timeline of the whole history of nuclear **proliferation**, plus which countries have nuclear weapons and how many, as well as their effects on people and the environment, and other useful information, take a look at the website of the International Campaign to Abolish Nuclear Weapons. http://www.icanw.org/the-facts/the-nuclear-age/

In 1960, France started a programme of testing, detonating its first nuclear device in the Sahara desert. This would lead directly to that fateful night in 1985 when the Rainbow Warrior was bombed.

EFFECTS OF A 100-KT NUCLEAR BOMB

3 km radius A radioactive fireball hotter than the Sun and with the force of 100,000 tonnes of TNT kills everyone.

5 km radius The vast majority of people die quickly from blast injuries, asphyxiation (suffocation) or (over weeks) radiation sickness.

10 km radius About half die from trauma and burns. Many succumb soon after to fires and radiation sickness.

80 km radius Radioactive fallout spreads. Over time, many thousands will die from radiation sickness and cancers.

It takes around 10 seconds for the fireball from a nuclear explosion to reach its maximum size, but the effects last for decades.

BLAST, HEAT AND RADIATION[#165]

A nuclear explosion releases vast amounts of energy in the form of blast, heat and radiation. An enormous shockwave reaches speeds of many hundreds of kilometres an hour. The blast kills people close to **ground zero**, and causes lung injuries, ear damage and internal bleeding further away. People sustain injuries from collapsing buildings and flying objects. Thermal radiation is so intense that almost everything close to ground zero is vaporized. The extreme heat causes severe burns and ignites fires over a large area, which combine into a giant firestorm. Even people in underground shelters face likely death due to a lack of oxygen and carbon monoxide poisoning.

RADIATION

Unlike conventional weapons, nuclear weapons release ionizing radiation: particles and rays given off by radioactive materials. At high doses, radiation kills cells, damages organs and causes rapid death. At low doses, it can damage cells and lead to cancer, genetic damage and mutations. In human beings, it causes most types of leukaemia, or blood cancer, as well as solid cancers such as thyroid, lung and breast cancers.

Increased rates of leukaemia and thyroid cancer among exposed children begin to appear after five years, while the incidence of most solid cancers rises after about 10 years, with the increased risk persisting throughout one's life. Radiation exposure can also heighten the risk of hereditary effects in future generations. Radiation exposure can occur externally (from particles in the air, water and soil) or internally (from breathing, eating and drinking). Many radioisotopes are concentrated in plants and animals, and thus the food chain.

NZ POST NUCLEAR-FREE STAMP

PROTEST MARCH AGAINST FRENCH NUCLEAR TESTING IN THE PACIFIC, WILLIS ST, WELLINGTON, 1972

1951: In the wake of World War II, Aotearoa/New Zealand and Australia align with the United States to form *the ANZUS Treaty*. With the signing of this, we accepted the protection of the United States so-called 'Nuclear Umbrella', meaning that we agreed to the possible use of the United States nuclear-powered vessels or weapons in the event of any attack on us.

1959: *The New Zealand Campaign for Nuclear Disarmament (CND) Movement* is co-founded in Christchurch with the help of **Elsie Locke** and **Mary Woodward**. It was largely from CND(NZ) and another community-led organisation, Peace Media, that Greenpeace NZ evolved.

1960: The first nuclear powered vessel to visit New Zealand arrives, the nuclear submarine USS Halibut. Its presence here is justified as meeting our obligations under the ANZUS Treaty.

1961: Marches take place in centres throughout the country to mark the first Hiroshima Day commemoration.

1963: A CND-initiated petition titled '*No Bombs South of the Line*' is signed by 80,000 people. It calls for a nuclear-free southern hemisphere.

1964: France shifts its nuclear testing from the Algerian Sahara to Mururoa Atoll in French Polynesia.

MATIU RATA

TIMELINE

NZ Prime Minister Norman Kirk said at the time: *'I believe that to base our foreign policies on moral principles is the most enlightened form of self-interest. What is morally right is likely to be politically right.'*

1972: By now anger over the French testing in the Pacific is widespread in Aotearoa/New Zealand. The 38ft ketch *Vega*, flying a Greenpeace banner, sets sail for Mururoa, captained by one of Greenpeace's founders, David McTaggart. Several other Aotearoa/New Zealand yachts join him, including one which carries Māori MP for Northland and Cabinet Minister Matiu Rata (the man largely responsible for the establishment of the Waitangi Tribunal in 1975), who later says: *'We represented small people from small countries who felt powerless in the face of events beyond the comprehension of our own government.'* Meanwhile, 10,000 people sign a petition calling for a halt to all French nuclear testing in the South Pacific.

1973: The *Vega* again sails into the test zone. The French Navy board the yacht and beat up captain David McTaggart. The photos go viral. Meanwhile, the Aotearoa/New Zealand and Australian Governments take France to the World Court over continued atmospheric testing. The Government sends the frigate *Otago*, and then the *Canterbury*, to the test zone, accompanied by the *HMAS Supply*, a fleet oiler of the Royal Australian Navy. Other Aotearoa/New Zealand yachts, including the *Fri*, *Spirit of Peace, Boy Roel, Magic Island* and the *Tanmure* also set sail in protest.

1974: Greenpeace New Zealand is officially founded.

1976: The new National Government announces it will welcome nuclear-powered and nuclear-armed warships. There are massive street marches in response. The USS Truxton is brought to a halt by a spectacular protest fleet of 80 vessels, and the public protest the visit of the USS Long Beach.

MEMBERS OF THE CAMPAIGN AGAINST NUCLEAR WARSHIPS (CANWAR) STAND ABOARD THE YACHT PHOENIX IN WELLINGTON HARBOUR WHILE AWAITING THE ARRIVAL OF THE USS LONG BEACH IN 1976

1978: Public protests are held against the visit of USS Pintado. There is deep concern over the risks posed by this technology. A new campaign starts to declare cars, houses, boroughs and city council areas nuclear-free zones.

1979: Public protests are held against the visit of USS Haddo. Between 1978 and 1983 the public opposition to nuclear-powered or armed ships rises from 32% to 72%.

1983: Auckland sees the biggest anti-nuclear march to date when 25,000 women march up Queen St.

1984: Election year in Aotearoa/New Zealand. As the election approaches, under intense public pressure, the Labour party commits itself to work actively for a nuclear-free Pacific, to ban nuclear-powered or nuclear weapon carrying ships, and to renegotiate the ANZUS Treaty. The US decide to test the resolve of the new Labour Government to move towards a Nuclear Free NZ by requesting permission for the ship USS Buchanan to visit. David Lange, the new Prime Minister shows he means business by saying 'No.' As a result, Washington severs all visible military ties with Aotearoa/New Zealand and downgrades all diplomatic and political exchanges. US Secretary of State, George Shultz, confirms it will no longer guarantee security to Aotearoa/New Zealand, although the ANZUS Treaty stays in place.

1985: The Greenpeace flagship, Rainbow Warrior is bombed and a crew member is murdered by French Government secret agents. Prime Minister David Lange argues that *'nuclear weapons are morally indefensible'* in a widely televised Oxford Union Debate in England, drawing thunderous applause when he quips in reply to an American student: *'Hold your breath for just a moment. I can smell the uranium on it as you lean toward me.'*

'There's only one thing worse than being incinerated by your enemies, and that's being incinerated by your friends.' David Lange.

LANGE WITH THE BILL TO DECLARE NEW ZEALAND NUCLEAR-FREE IN 1985.

1987: The *New Zealand Free Zone, Disarmament and Arms Control Act* comes into force, making Aotearoa/New Zealand a nuclear-free nation. In response, the US Congress retaliates with the *Broomfield Act*, downgrading Aotearoa/New Zealand's status from 'ally' to 'friend'.

1989: 52% of Aotearoa/New Zealanders indicate they'd rather break defence ties with the US than admit nuclear-armed ships into our waters.

1990: Prior to the national election, the National Party commits itself to keep Aotearoa/New Zealand nuclear-free.

1994: Aotearoa/New Zealand is the only Western Nation to vote in favour of the resolution before the UN General Assembly asking for an advisory ruling on the legality of the threat of use, or use of nuclear weapons.

1995: On the eve of the 10th anniversary of the Rainbow Warrior bombing, and the anniversary of Hiroshima and Nagasaki, French President Jacques Chirac announces the resumption of nuclear testing at Moruroa. A massive flotilla leaves from Aotearoa/New Zealand to protest. Two Greenpeace ships are arrested. All political parties declare unanimous opposition to French nuclear testing.

1996: The International Court of Justice gives its advisory opinion on the general illegality of nuclear weapons.

1997: The *Model Nuclear Weapons Convention* is drafted under the name of the Lawyers' Committee on Nuclear Policy and circulated by the UN Secretary-General as a UN document (one of the two drafters is Aotearoa/New Zealander, Alyn Ware).

1998: Foreign ministers from eight countries, including Aotearoa/New Zealand's Foreign Minister, release a declaration calling for a new agenda for nuclear disarmament.

1999: A group of Aotearoa/New Zealanders participate in the historic *Hague Appeal for Peace Conference*.

2000: The *Nuclear Non-Proliferation Treaty Review Conference* adopts 13 steps for nuclear disarmament by consensus, including the nuclear weapon nations. Aotearoa/New Zealand Disarmament Ambassador Clive Pearson chairs the sub-committee responsible for negotiating these steps.

2002: Aotearoa/New Zealand section of the *Parliamentary Network for Nuclear Disarmament* is established.

BUT WHAT ABOUT NUCLEAR POWER GENERATION? ISN'T THAT THE WAY OF THE FUTURE?

Currently Aotearoa/New Zealand's Nuclear Free policy also includes a ban on the use of nuclear power. But nuclear power can generate electricity without greenhouse gas emissions, produces low-cost electricity and doesn't rely on fossil fuels, so why is there still concern about it?

Extremely costly to build. According to the *Union of Concerned Scientists*, the first nuclear power plants built proved so expensive to build that *'half of them were abandoned during construction. Those that were completed saw huge cost overruns, which were passed on to utility customers in the form of rate increases. By 1985, Forbes had labelled US nuclear power "the largest managerial disaster in business history".'* Spiralling, inexact costing continues to be a problem for nuclear power in the 21st century. *'Between 2002 and 2008, for example, cost estimates for new nuclear plant construction rose from between $2 billion and $4 billion per unit to $9 billion per unit, according to a 2009 UCS report, while experience with new construction in Europe has seen costs continue to soar.'*[#167] As well, there are the huge costs of containing the radioactive waste (see below).

Currently not renewable. Nuclear energy is not a renewable resource. Uranium, the nuclear fuel used to produce nuclear power, is limited and can't be reused. It's estimated that with the current global rate of consumption of uranium, there is only enough for another 70-80 years.[#168]

Environmental Impact: There are huge environmental and health impacts from mining and refining uranium. According to a 2008 article in The Guardian newspaper,[#169] *'to produce the 25 tonnes or so of uranium fuel needed to keep your average reactor going for a year entails the extraction of half a million tonnes of waste rock and over 100,000 tonnes of mill tailings. Contamination of local water supplies around uranium mines and processing plants has been documented in Brazil, Colorado, Texas, Australia, Namibia and many other sites. To supply even a fraction of the power stations the industry expects to be online worldwide in 2020 would mean generating 50 million tonnes of toxic radioactive residues every single year.'* It goes on to say: *'The World Nuclear Association (WNA), the trade body for companies that make up 90% of the industry, admits that in "emerging uranium producing countries" there is frequently no adequate environmental health and safety legislation, let alone monitoring. As well, transporting nuclear fuel to and from plants represents a **pollution hazard**.'* Perhaps worst of all, once the fuel is used, you can't simply take it to the landfill – it's radioactive and dangerous.

Radioactive Waste Disposal: As a rule, a nuclear power plant creates 20 metric tons of nuclear fuel per year, and with that comes a lot of nuclear waste. When you consider the combined number of nuclear plants, that number jumps to approximately 2,000 metric tons a year. Most of this waste emits radiation and creates high temperatures, suggesting that it might eventually destroy any compartment that contains it. Used nuclear fuel decays to safe radioactive levels over time — however, even low-level radioactive waste takes **hundreds of years** to reach acceptably safe levels.

Nuclear Accidents: The radioactive waste produced can pose serious health effects on the lives of people as well as the environment. High profile disasters in **Chernobyl,** Ukraine, in 1986, and **Fukushima**, Japan, in 2011, have raised public awareness of the dangers of nuclear power. Meltdowns like these released enormous amounts of radiation into the surrounding communities, forcing hundreds of thousands of people to evacuate, with many possibly never able to return. The accident at the Chernobyl Nuclear Power Plant has been called the worst to date, with several scientists now linking it to some 985,000 human deaths between when the accident occurred in 1986 and 2004, mainly from cancer.[170] More deaths, they project, will follow.

The Fukushima disaster, the result of the power plant being destroyed by the 2011 Tōhoku earthquake and tsunami, is still thought to be leaking radiative waste into the oceans, which goes on to be distributed by currents all around the Pacific. The Japanese government has now *'been obliged to acknowledge that the severity rating of its nuclear crisis … matches that of the 1986 Chernobyl disaster.'* [171]

*"**Hazardous radioactive** elements being released in the sea and air around Fukushima accumulate at each step of various food chains (for example, into algae, crustaceans, small fish, bigger fish, then humans; or soil, grass, cow's meat and milk, then humans). Entering the body, these elements – called internal emitters – migrate to specific organs such as the thyroid, liver, bone, and brain, continuously irradiating small volumes of cells with high doses of alpha, beta and/or gamma radiation, and over many years often induce cancer".* [172]

Hot Target for Terrorists: Nuclear energy has immense power. There is some concern that nuclear power plants could become a target of a terrorist attack by damaging or destroying the nuclear facility, causing the population to be exposed to radiation.

WHAT BECAME OF THE RAINBOW WARRIOR?

After a hui was held in Matauri Bay (north of the *Bay of Islands*), Ngāti Kura (a hapu of Ngapuhi) and Greenpeace agreed to bury the Rainbow Warrior at sea, so the wreck would be an underwater memorial for use by divers. On the 2nd of December, 1987, the hull of the Rainbow Warrior was temporarily patched and the ship was towed to a site just off Matauri Bay, near the Cavalli Islands. This site was chosen because it had enough depth for other vessels to pass safely overhead, while still accessible to underwater divers and protected from the worst of the sea-swell. On the 12th of December it was given a traditional Māori burial and the sea-cocks were then opened while well-wishers watched from both land and sea. Since then the wreck has become a living reef, popular to divers from all around the world.

UNDERWATER VIEW OF RAINBOW WARRIOR.

A CLOSER LOOK: THE FRENCH TESTS AT MURUROA

The first French nuclear tests took place in the Algerian Sahara, while it was still under French rule. As soon as Algeria was granted independence in 1962, it banned nuclear testing there and the tests were moved to Mururoa Atoll (historically known as Aopuni) and its sister atoll Fangataufa, in the Taumotu Archipelago of French-controlled Polynesia in the southern Pacific Ocean. The atoll of Hao, 450 kilometres north-west of Mururoa, was used as a support base for the tests and other operations.

The first test was code-named 'Aldebaran' after a giant orange star located about 65 light years from the Sun. It was conducted on July 2, 1966, despite objections from 30 members of the Polynesian Territorial Assembly. Greenpeace observers described how the explosion sucked all the water out of the lagoon, '*raining dead fish and molluscs down on the atoll*' and spreading contamination across the Pacific as far as Aotearoa/New Zealand and Peru.[173]

Ignoring international criticism, the French government carried out an estimated 193 to 198 nuclear tests on Moruroa and Fangataufa between 1966 and 1996: 41–44 atmospheric tests and approximately 154 underground tests (the exact number is still classified information).[174]

The first bombs were detonated on boats in the lagoon but caused such high radioactive fallout that the following tests used warheads hanging under balloons. As a result of huge international protests, after 1974 the tests were then moved into deep shafts dug into the atoll's rocky volcanic core. But controversy continued, as the underground explosions cracked the atolls. It was feared the radiative material trapped beneath would escape and contaminate the surrounding ocean and neighbouring atolls, in what was known as 'tired mountain syndrome.'

According to the *International Physicians for the Prevention of Nuclear War* (IPPNW), '*during the three decades of testing, about 5,000 people lived within a 1,000 km radius of the nuclear test site. The atolls of Mangareva and Tureia, 100 km away, were most severely affected by radioactive fallout and had to be evacuated due to high levels of radiation in 1968. Several accidents added to the radioactive exposure of the population. In July 1966, a nuclear bomb broke apart on the surface of Moruroa, dispersing large amounts of plutonium-239.*'[175] In July 1979, a 120 kiloton nuclear detonation was conducted at half the usual depth, when the nuclear device got stuck halfway down the 800 metre shaft.[176] This caused an underwater landslide on Moruroa, which released huge amounts of radioactivity into the ocean and triggered a tsunami, injuring workers and '*wreaking havoc on many islands in the archipelago.*'[177] A 2 km long by 40 cm wide crack appeared on the atoll as a result of the blast. '*In the spring of 1981, cyclones hit Moruroa, washing radioactive waste into the ocean, including much of the plutonium released in 1966.*'[178]

When French President Jacques Chirac decided to run a series of nuclear tests at Mururoa between 5th Sept and 2nd October 1995 (just one year before the Comprehensive Test Ban Treaty was due to be signed) there was a world-wide protest. There were **boycotts** on French wine, riots across Polynesia, and talk of cutting France out of any meetings related to the South Pacific. The last test was detonated on 27 January 1996, with the French government leaving a monitoring system in place to keep a watch on the lingering radiation and the state of the atoll. According to one report, only 11 of the original 20

LEFT: FRENCH NUCLEAR TESTING BASE ON MORUROA ATOLL

BELOW: A NUCLEAR BOMB EXPLOSION, OFTEN CALLED A 'MUSHROOM'

system sensors are still working, meaning the atoll could potentially collapse without any warning.[#179]

Michael Field, a Pacific reporter wrote on the issue in 2013, '*radiation levels frequently rose in New Zealand 4700 kms away following each test*'. He said the residual mass of plutonium 239 (about 500 kilos) was '*extremely toxic and has to be contained for 240,000 years before it can enter the wider environment*'[#180] safely.

In 1998, the French Defence Minister admitted that the population of the islands of Tureia, Reao, Pukarua, Mangareva and Tahiti were also affected by radioactive fallout from the nuclear tests, along with the soldiers and civilians who worked on them.[#181] One veteran described how he was stationed in shorts and T-shirts on a boat only 24 kms from the explosion before being sent into the immediate area of the mushroom cloud to check the damage.[#182]

In November 2008, France's Defence Minister, Hervé Morin, announced that a law would be introduced to **compensate** those suffering illness relating to the tests, including the 150,000 army and civilians who worked on the tests in Algeria and the French-controlled Polynesian atolls. '*Today, we must recognise these victims,*' he said.[#183]

But, although France finally passed the law in 2010, the way it was worded excluded many from any hope for compensation. Undeterred, Richard Tuheiava, a member of the French Polynesian Assembly, kept pushing and said the effects were clear. '*The fact is since the [tests] … most of the diseases are cancer and leukaemia … a result of the nuclear testing.*'[#184] Scientific studies have backed this claim, suggesting increased rates of cancer in those exposed to radiation.

In 2014, Mr Tuheiava led a move to ask France for close to US$1 billion compensation for environmental damage, as well as for the French military's continued occupation of Mururoa and Fangataufa (which are still uninhabitable), and to help pay for ongoing healthcare needs. However, though the French President François Hollande made promises to finally "*turn the Pg on the issue of nuclear testing*"[#185] in 2016, the president of the Nuclear Workers' Association said little had come of that, and the people were fast tiring of broken and unfulfilled promises from Paris.[#186] That same year, a report from Radio NZ said that of more than 1,000 claims, only 19 people have ever received compensation.[#187] It seems that, even now, over 50 years since the first nuclear test at Mururoa, the fight for full justice for those affected still continues.

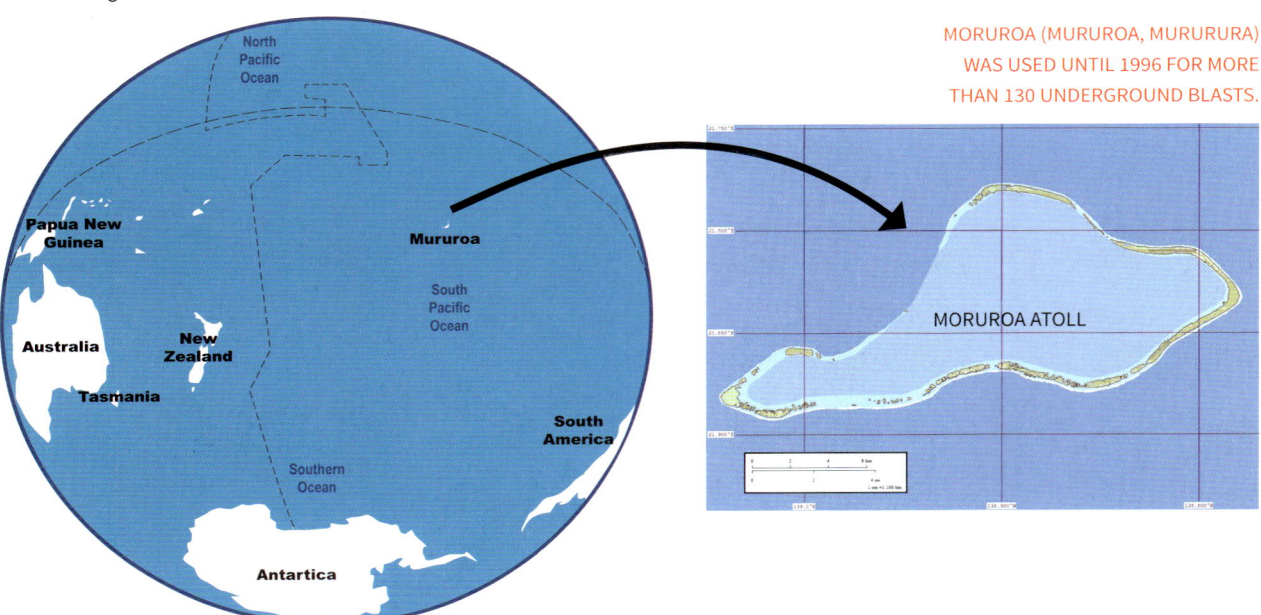

MORUROA (MURUROA, MURURURA) WAS USED UNTIL 1996 FOR MORE THAN 130 UNDERGROUND BLASTS.

FROM OUT OF THE PAST...
THE SPIES SPEAK:[188]

Colonel Jean Luc Kister

TVNZ ONE-NEWS, RAINBOW WARRIOR BOMBER BREAKS HIS SILENCE AFTER 30 YEARS.

In 2015, TVNZ's '*Sunday*' programme tracked down one of the French secret agents who had planted the bomb on the *Rainbow Warrior*. Colonel Jean Luc Kister, who led the dive team, told them: '*For us it was just like using boxing gloves in order to crush a mosquito. It was a disproportionate operation, but we had to obey the order, we were soldiers.*' He said that though they had succeed in sinking the Rainbow Warrior, the operation was a '*big fail*' and the aim of the mission was '*not to injure anyone.*'

'*We are not assassins and we have a conscience. I have the weight of an innocent's man's death on my conscience . . . It's time, I believe, for me to express my profound regret and my apologies.*'
J L Kister

Christine Cabon (alias Frederique Bonlieu)

CHRISTINE CABON, NOW AND THEN.

Cabon, who infiltrated Greenpeace, and pretended to support them, was tracked down to a small village in the south of France in 2017, where she lives with her four dogs and spends her time as an historian and local councillor. At the time of the bombing she vanished without a trace. When confronted, she initially refused to speak about the bombing, before saying '*I think all military people who serve their countries can find themselves in situations they hadn't wished for.*' Unlike Kister, she did not apologise, though admitted '*there was nothing glamourous about the life of a notorious spy*'.

'*To New Zealanders, we are the terrorists.*'
C. Cabon

ARE WE THERE YET? HOW HAS THIS EVENT HELPED SHAPE AOTEAROA/NEW ZEALAND SOCIETY?

Rather than achieving Operation Satanic's ultimate goal of halting the protests against France's nuclear tests, the sinking of the Rainbow Warrior, and its aftermath, set in motion a significant shift in Aotearoa/New Zealand society and the way we viewed ourselves in the larger world. It hardened our attitudes to all things nuclear — culminating in our Nuclear-Free status — and changed our relationship with our military allies to this day.

Most Aotearoa/New Zealanders proudly talk about how we 'stood up to the Big Boys' and marked out an independent foreign policy path. Our stance as a 'plucky' little Pacific nation sees us roundly oppose weapons of mass destruction, and support calls for nuclear disarmament. We view ourselves as promoters of peace on the world's stage. We also continue to resist the arguments for nuclear power, instead building on our image of a peaceful, 'clean green' country.

In 2001 the Ministry for the Environment commissioned research to estimate what our 'clean green' image is worth, polling key export customers. It found that this image has '*significant export value. Our environmental image is a key driver of the value of goods and services in the international market place.*' #189 Part of this image, certainly, is our stand as a nuclear-free nation.

The protests and trauma triggered by the Rainbow Warrior bombing have also impacted on our shared cultural identity. It was, perhaps, the first time many Pākehā Aotearoa/New Zealanders saw themselves as part of a wider Pacific community, breaking down cultural barriers to fight on behalf of our Pacific cousins against a threat that could ultimately endanger us all. As with the other pivotal moments in Aotearoa/New Zealand history explored in this book, part of this story is about the 'people power' that eventually convinced politicians to answer their citizens' call for change. This is the way a healthy democracy should work: *a government of the people, by the people, for the people,* as described by Abraham Lincoln, 16th President of the United States. The heroes here are the thousands of Aotearoa/New Zealanders who marched, signed petitions, put their lives at risk out on the water, supported antinuclear, environmental and peace organisations, and refused to give up. Future generations, living more safely as a result, have a lot to be thankful for. It's now up to us to keep this flame of true democracy, environmental safety, and peace brightly burning.

That said, just as past governments supported the protests against the French testing at Mururoa, so, too, government actions can work to undermine protest. In 2013, the National-led government passed *the Crown Minerals Amendment Act 2013* under 'urgency', meaning there was no opportunity for the public to have their say, nor any scrutiny by a select committee. Designed to protect overseas interests as they search for oil and gas in our territorial waters, Clause 14 extends a 'no protest' zone put in place by the National government's previous '*Anadarko Bill*' much further out to sea — 350 nautical miles from our coastline. This Act curtails people's democratic right to protest and, though a Greenpeace petition got tens of thousands of signatures objecting to it, the government slipped this new law through.

Greenpeace Executive Director Bunny McDiarmid called that law, "*an affront to New Zealand democracy, and to our long held right and proud tradition of peaceful protest at sea.*"#190 Put to the test in 2017, Greenpeace NZ's Executive Director Russel Norman and climate activist, Sara Howell, were charged under the Act over a protest against deep-water seismic testing off the Wairarapa coast, facing the possibility of up to one year in jail and fines of $50,000 if found guilty.[191] On the 21st September 2018, they were discharged without conviction at the Napier District Court.

"We're thrilled with this verdict. We see this as a major win not just for us, but for the whole movement of people fighting against fossil fuels," Norman said. [192]

DID YOU KNOW?
Several NZ songwriters, writers, film-makers and artists have used the Rainbow Warrior incident and French testing as the subject of their work. How many can you find?

RAINBOW WARRIOR, 1985 IN AUCKLAND

AN EXCELLENT COLLECTION OF RESOURCES CAN BE FOUND HERE:
https://www.greenpeace.org/new-zealand/about/our-history/bombing-of-the-rainbow-warrior/the-bombing-of-the-rainbow-warrior-fact-file/#background-to-the-bombing

A range of well-known Aotearoa/New Zealand groups and individuals slammed the government's controversial move to criminalise aspects of peaceful protests at sea. In a joint statement, Greenpeace, Rt Hon Geoffrey Palmer QC, Peter Williams QC, WWF, Forest and Bird, Dame Anne Salmond, Rikirangi Gage of Te Whānau-ā-Apanui, Sir Ngatata Love, the New Zealand Council of Trade Unions, George Armstrong (founder of the Peace Squadron), Amnesty International NZ, actress Lucy Lawless and many others, said '*the new law is a sledgehammer designed to attack peaceful protest*' and is '*being bundled through Parliament without proper scrutiny despite its significant constitutional, democratic and human rights implications.*'[192]

Whether the Labour-led coalition government who took power in 2017 will revise this, is still unknown. But, if this story teaches us nothing else, as Desmond Tutu [193] once said, the price of freedom is eternal vigilance. Watch this space!

> 'At the heart of the idea of democracy is the notion that people's engagement in public life is fundamentally a force for good which leads to the betterment of society.' Helen Clark, former Aotearoa/New Zealand Prime Minister: Statement at 2015 International Day of Democracy ' Space for Civil Society'.

REFERENCES

THE FOLLOWING SOURCES WERE REFERED TO IN THE PREPARATION OF THIS TEXT.

EXTRAORDINARY WOMEN, THE STORY OF AOTEAROA/NEW ZEALAND WOMEN'S RIGHT TO VOTE:

#1 Robert McCrum 17 Jul 2017, The Guardian https://www.theguardian.com/books/2017/jul/17/100-best-nonfiction-books-vindication-rights-woman-mary-wollstonecraft

#4 Raewyn Dalziel. 'Müller, Mary Anne', *Dictionary of New Zealand Biography*, first published in 1990. Te Ara - the Encyclopedia of New Zealand, https://teara.govt.nz/en/biographies/1m59/muller-mary-anne (accessed 13 February 2018)

#5 Quote: https://teara.govt.nz/en/biographies/2c25/colclough-mary-ann

#6 https://teara.govt.nz/en/biographies/2m30/mangakahia-meri-te-tai

#9 https://www.nzedge.com/legends/kate-sheppard/

#10 NZ Herald, 8 March 1887, p. 6

#11 http://www.nzedge.com/legends/kate-sheppard/

#12 Video on https://www.youtube.com/watch?v=6dN6fhY-CrBU

https://teara.govt.nz/en including:
- #3 https://teara.govt.nz/en/biographies/1m59/muller-mary-anne
- #6 https://teara.govt.nz/en/biographies/2m30/mangakahia-meri-te-tai
- #8 Angela Ballara. 'Ratana, Iriaka Matiu', Dictionary of New Zealand Biography, first published in 2000. Te Ara - the Encyclopedia of New Zealand, https://teara.govt.nz/en/biographies/5r7/ratana-iriaka-matiu (accessed 2 October 2018)
- #9 Megan Cook, 'Divorce and separation - Growth in divorce: 1898–1979', Te Ara - the Encyclopedia of New Zealand, http://www.TeAra.govt.nz/en/divorce-and-separation/Pg-2 (accessed 2 October 2018)

The NZ History website from the Ministry for Culture and Heritage https://nzhistory.govt.nz/ including:
- #2 'Women's suffrage milestones ', URL: https://nzhistory.govt.nz/politics/womens-suffrage/suffrage-milestones, (Ministry for Culture and Heritage), updated 13-Jan-2016
- #7 https://nzhistory.govt.nz/people/niniwa-heremaia

New Zealand Electronic Text Collection http://nzetc.victoria.ac.nz/tm/scholarly/name-457099.html

The National Library and ATL Collections https://natlib.govt.nz/collections

Archives NZ http://archives.govt.nz/

Te Ara – The Encyclopaedia of New Zealand and Dictionary of New Zealand Biography Universal Franchise In New Zealand https://simranwomenssuffrage.weebly.com/

THE GREAT DIVIDE, 1981 SPRINGBOK TOUR:

#13 *By Batons and Barbed Wire – A Response to the 1981 Springbok Tour of New Zealand*, Tom Newnham, Graphic Publications Ltd., 1983.

#14 Parliamentary Debates, Volume 439

#15 First coined by settler, Charles Hursthouse, in his book *New Zealand, the Britain of the South*, 1875

#17 *Dictionary of South African Quotations*, Jennifer Crwys-Williams, Penguin Books 1994, p207.

#18 Statstics drawn from:
- https://en.wikipedia.org/wiki/Demographics_of_South_Africa
- Smuts I: The Sanguine Years 1870–1919, W.K. Hancock, Cambridge University Press, 1962, pg 219
- Europa Year Book 1969, Volume II: Africa, The Americas, Asia, Australasia, Europa Publications, London, 1969, Pg 1286

#19 Africa :: SOUTH AFRICA. CIA The World Factbook.

#22 Refer to the chapter on Pg 64, for an unsettling comparison.

#23 Sunday Times, November 2006, 5, via https://quotesss.com/quote/978889

#24 16 June 1976 Student Uprising in Soweto. africanhistory.about.com; Harrison, David (1987). The White Tribe of Africa; Elsabe Brink; Gandhi Malungane; Steve Lebelo; Dumisani Ntshangase; Sue Krige, Soweto 16 June, 1976 9, 2001; Les Payne writing in Newsday.

#25 http://www.mandela.gov.za/mandela_speeches/941003/1994_unga.htm

#26 http://www.un.org/en/universal-declaration-human-rights/

#28 Trevor Richards, *Dancing on our bones: New Zealand, South Africa, rugby and racism*. Wellington: Bridget Williams Books, 1999, p. 12.

#29 R. Thompson, *Retreat from apartheid – New Zealand's sporting contacts with South Africa*. Dunedin: Otago University Press, 1975, p. 12.

#30 #31 Robert Consedine Anti-racism and the Treaty of Waitangi. https://teara.govt.nz/en/anti-racism-and-treaty-of-waitangi-activism

#32 #36 *The Gleneagles Agreement on Sporting Contacts with South Africa* (PDF). London: Commonwealth. 1977.

#37 *Gleneagles Agreement*, URL: https://nzhistory.govt.nz/culture/-1981springbok-tour/gleneagles-agreement, (Ministry for Culture and Heritage), updated -13Jan2016-

#40 Equates to a general increase in prices and a fall in the purchasing value/power of money.

#41 http://www.wcl.govt.nz/heritage/tour.html

#45 https://teara.govt.nz/en/nga-ropu-tautohetohe-maori-protest-movements/Pg4-

#46 http://www.nzherald.co.nz/nz/news/article.cfm?c_id=1&objectid=10391310

#47 http://www.stuff.co.nz/taranaki-daily-news/news/8998870/Kiwi-speak

#50 Sourced from the Security Intelligence Service

#51 http://www.nickyhager.info/a-short-history-of-the-new-zealand-security-intelligence-service-nzsis/

#58 https://rdln.wordpress.com/15/07/2011/greater-even-than-rugby-the-1981-springbok-tour/

#63 https://www.sahistory.org.za/people/pieter-willem-botha

#64 https://www.nelsonmandela.org/content/Pg/biography

#66 http://www.mandela.gov.za/mandela_speeches/951115/1995_newzealand.htm

#70 http://www.marxist.com/new-zealand-the-silent-revolution-springbok-tour.htm

#71 https://www.nzonscreen.com/title/patu1983-

#72 http://www.mandela.gov.za/mandela_speeches/050203/2005_poverty.htm

The NZ History website from the Ministry for Culture and Heritage https://nzhistory.govt.nz/ including:

- #15 https://nzhistory.govt.nz/culture/1981-springbok-tour/impact-of-the-tour
- #27 https://nzhistory.govt.nz/culture/1981-springbok-tour/politics-and-sport
- #33 #35 'Stopping the 1973 tour', URL: https://nzhistory.govt.nz/culture/1981-springbok-tour/1973-springbok-tour, (Ministry for Culture and Heritage), updated 13-Aug-2014
- #34 #38 https://nzhistory.govt.nz/culture/1981-springbok-tour
- #39 https://nzhistory.govt.nz/culture/1981-springbok-tour/battle-lines-are-drawn
- #55 https://nzhistory.govt.nz/culture/1981-springbok-tour/tour-diary
- #49 'Police baton anti-tour protesters outside Parliament', URL: https://nzhistory.govt.nz/police-baton-anti-spring-bok-tour-protestors-near-parliament, (Ministry for Culture and Heritage), updated 24-Jul-2017
- #57 https://nzhistory.govt.nz/media/interactive/interac-tive-springbok-tour-schedule

Wikipedia, including:

- #21 https://en.wikipedia.org/wiki/Apartheid https://en.wikipedia.org/wiki/Apartheid
- #67 https://en.wikipedia.org/wiki/New_Zealand_Cavaliers
- #62 https://en.wikipedia.org/wiki/1981_South_Africa_rugby_union_tour_of_New_Zealand_and_the_United_States

News Reports, including:

- #20 https://www.news24.com/MyNews24/Black-Apart-heid-Legacy-The-untold-stories-of-the-Rainbow-Na-tion-20130818
- #42 #43 #44 Redmer Yska / 09 July, 2011 https://www.noted.co.nz/archive/listener-nz-2011/inside-the-1981-springbok-tour/
- #48 http://www.stuff.co.nz/dominion-post/capital-life/8998581/The-night-of-the-batons-still-defiant-30-years-on
- #52 https://www.nytimes.com/1981/08/15/sports/bomb-explodes-near-springboks-game-site.html
- #53 https://www.noted.co.nz/archive/listener-nz-2011/inside-the-1981-springbok-tour/
- #54 #56 #61 https://www.pressreader.com/new-zealand/the-press/20110730/282948151899308

- #59 #60 http://www.nzherald.co.nz/nz/news/article.cfm?c_id=1&objectid=206678
- #65 https://www.independent.co.uk/news/world/africa/jacob-zuma-corruption-charges-south-africa-presdent-arms-deal-a8291826.html
- #68 http://www.scoop.co.nz/stories/PO0607/S00145.htm
- #69 http://www.stuff.co.nz/blogs/opinion/2663799/A-battle-for-the-soul-of-New-Zealand

Te Ara – *The Encyclopaedia of New Zealand and Dictionary of New Zealand Biography*

RACISM NEVER SLEEPS, THE DAWN RAIDS:

Immigration and National Identity in 1970s New Zealand. James Mitchell, University of Otago, 2003
#75 #77 #80 #81 #86 #119 #130

- #82 Page 148 of above reference
- #85 Page 134 Table 2
- #95 Page 22 Ross
- #96 Page 148,149 and transcript of https://www.nzonscreen.com/title/dawn-raids-2005
- #99 #122 Page 239
- #100 Page 62 Ross
- #101 Page 241-242
- #105 Pages 150-157
- #112 #113 Pages 152-153
- #120 Auckland Star 26/10/76
- #121 Page 255 Statistics derived from official estimate of overstayers from 1977
- #122 Page 239
- #125 #126 Page 144

Te Ara – *The Encyclopaedia of New Zealand and Dictionary of New Zealand Biography* https://teara.govt.nz/en including:

- #89 https://teara.govt.nz/en/pacific-islands-and-new-zealand/Pg-2
- #114 Paul Spoonley, 'Ethnic and religious intolerance - Anti-Asian politics', Te Ara - the Encyclopedia of New Zealand, http://www.TeAra.govt.nz/en/ethnic-and-religious-intolerance/page-5 (accessed 10 October 2018) and https://www.nzherald.co.nz/nz/news/article.cfm?c_id=1&objectid=10501783
- #152 Paul Spoonley, 'Ethnic and religious intolerance - Intolerance towards Pacific migrants', Te Ara - the Encyclopedia of New Zealand, http://www.TeAra.govt.nz/en/ethnic-and-religious-intolerance/Pg-4 https://teara.govt.nz/en/video/16199/bastion-point-protest
- #155 https://teara.govt.nz/en/pacific-arts-in-new-zealand/print

News Reports, including:

- #74 Dr Brian Edwards, speaking on television programme 'Compass 1968'
- #83 Truth newspaper editorial, 12/2/74
- #87 NZ Herald newspaper editorial 16/9/69
- #88 Katherine Findlay, 'A Second Migration', Listener 9/10/76, p. 21.
- #104 Memo Office of the Minister of Immigration to all districts, 9/10/74 in DOL 22/1/109-4. NZ Herald 10/7/74 p. 1
- #114 https://www.nzherald.co.nz/nz/news/article.cfm?c_id=1&objectid=10501783
- #124 NZ Herald 23/3/74, p. 6. Paper given by Clive Edwards at Inter-Church Committee on Immigration (ICCI) seminar, St Johns College Auckland, 10/4/76
- #120 #127 Auckland Star 26/10/76
- #129 Auckland Star 23/10/76 Quote from Pua Sofi, in MFAT 301/1/5pt.3
- #128 NZ Herald 13/11/76 p 1.
- #133 NZ Herald 22/6/01 *Polynesia's radical spirit* https://www.nzherald.co.nz/nz/news/article.cfm?c_id=1&objectid=196354
- #134 #135 NZ Herald *Brown Power* Catherine Masters http://www.nzherald.co.nz/nz/news/article.cfm?c_id=1&objectid=10391310
- #143 http://salient.org.nz/2010/05/how-the-polynesian-panthers-changed-our-world/
- #144 http://www.nzherald.co.nz/nz/news/article.cfm?c_id=1&objectid=11413079
- #151 NZ Herald article: Diverse: 13 Maori and Pacific ministers sworn into NZ Government, 26/10/17 https://www.nzherald.co.nz/nz/news/article.cfm?c_id=1&objectid=11937027
- #153 https://www.radionz.co.nz/news/national/354217/deportation-modelling-bringing-back-the-dawn-raids
- #154 https://www.radionz.co.nz/news/national/354553/immigration-minister-puts-controversial-profiling-programme-on-hold

Dawn Raids (directed by Damon Fepulea'I), Isola Productions 2005. https://www.nzonscreen.com/title/dawn-raids-2005

- #106 #107 #108 #109 #110 #136 #141 #145 #156

- #115 Newspaper headlines in this documentary
- #116 Transcribed from an interview.
- #117 Transcribed from an interview with Aussie Malcolm
- #118 Transcribed from an interview

#73 #76 http://archive.stats.govt.nz/browse_for_stats/people_and_communities/pacific_peoples/pacific-progress-demography/population-growth.aspx

#78 Paul Reeves, *South Pacific Year: Meeting Point '71: Five Discussions about Our Unique Social and Geographical Problems in 1971*, National Council of Churches, Christchurch, 1971, p. 17.

#79 Safe - a cupboard on the south-facing wall of a house with external mesh to keep food, drink and meat cool as an alternative to a fridge.

#84 Paul Spoonley, " „The Multi-Cultural Workforce: The Role of Employers as Gatekeepers, New Zealand Journal of Industrial Relations, v. 3, 1978, p. 65.

#88 https://en.wikipedia.org/wiki/Police_raid

#90 #91 Professor Paul Spoonley, Massey University, speaking in the documentary 'Dawn Raids' (directed by Damon Fepulea'I), Isola Productions 2005. https://www.nzonscreen.com/title/dawn-raids-2005

#92 A political football is a topic or issue that is seized on by opposing political parties or factions and made a more political issue than it might initially seem to be.' https://educalingo.com/en/dic-en/political-football

#93 W G Coppell, Problems of Polynesia's Biggest City, PIM, v. 45, no. 11, Nov. 74, pp. 35-6 .

#94 https://itstopswithme.humanrights.gov.au/what-can-you-do/speak/casual-racism

#97 *All Power To The People: Overstayers, Dawn Raids and the Polynesian Panthers* from Tangata O Le Moana: *New Zealand and the people of the pacific* , ed. Sean Mallon, Kolokesa Māhina-Tuai and Damon Salesa, p222 This 1968 amendment allowed for the deportation of those overstaying their work permits and for police to ask for proof of the correct visas and passports

#98 See the explanation of Pass Laws in the section on the 1981 Springbok Tour Page 36

#102 Page 227-30, Anae, Melanie (2012). 'Overstayers, Dawn Raids and the Polynesian Panthers'. In Sean, Mallon. *Tangata O Le Moana: New Zealand and the People of the Pacific*. Te Papa Press.

#103 Page 65, Ross as above.

#111 You can view part of the National Party TV advertisement at: **https://www.youtube.com/watch?v=e6-xc_Oq3io**

#123 Joris de Bres and Rob Campbell, *The Overstayers: Illegal Migration from the Pacific Islands to New Zealand*, Auckland Resource Centre for World Development, Auckland, 1976, pp. 20-1.

#131 #132 https://polynesianpantersparty.weebly.com/polynesian-panthers.html

#137 Find out more about this at https://teara.govt.nz/en/video/16199/bastion-point-protest and https://nzhistory.govt.nz/keyword/bastion-point

#138 Find out more about these protests at: https://nzhistory.govt.nz/keyword/waitangi-day and https://teara.govt.nz/en/nga-ropu-tautohetohe-maori-protest-movements/page-2

#139 #140 From: https://polynesianpantersparty.weebly.com/polynesian-panthers.html and 'Dawn Raids' (directed by Damon Fepulea'I), Isola Productions 2005. https://www.nzonscreen.com/title/dawn-raids-2005

#142 https://e-tangata.co.nz/news/will-ilolahia-once-a-panther-always-a-panther

#146 Refer the *1981 Springbok Tour* page 32

#147 https://e-tangata.co.nz/history/melani-anae-racism-was-all-around-us/

#148 http://archive.stats.govt.nz/Census/2013-census/profile-and-summary-reports/quickstats-culture-identity/pacific-peoples.aspx

#149 http://socialreport.msd.govt.nz/civil-and-political-rights/representation-of-ethnic-groups-in-government.html

#150 https://www.parliament.nz/resource/en-NZ/00PLLawRP17041/4107f6fef63135f9e2e297af9318a7edf69cd3c3

The NZ History website from the Ministry for Culture and Heritage https://nzhistory.govt.nz/ including:

https://nzhistory.govt.nz/keyword/bastion-point

https://nzhistory.govt.nz/keyword/waitangi-day

SHIPS, SPIES & SABOTAGE, THE BOMBING OF THE RAINBOW WARRIOR:

Greenpeace website, including:

- #157 https://www.greenpeace.org/archive-international/en/about/history/mejato/
- #160 https://www.greenpeace.org/archive-international/en/about/history/the-bombing-of-the-rainbow-war/rainbow/The-crew-then-and-now/

- #161 http://www.greenpeace.org/new-zealand/en/about/history/The-bombing-of-the-Rainbow-Warrior-/Timeline-The-bombing-of-the-Rainbow-Warrior/
- #166 Timeline adapted from http://www.greenpeace.org/new-zealand/en/campaigns/nuclear/nuclear-free-nz/anti-nuke-history-NZ/
- #190 #191 http://www.greenpeace.org/new-zealand/en/press/Government-Bid-to-Criminalise-Sea-Protests-Slammed/

News Reports, including:

- #158 http://www.stuff.co.nz/sunday-star-times/features/3975978/The-deadly-fallout
- #192 https://www.nzherald.co.nz/business/news/article.cfm?c_id=3&objectid=12129463
- #169 https://www.theguardian.com/commentisfree/2008/dec/05/nuclear-greenpolitics
- #182 https://www.theguardian.com/world/2013/jul/03/french-nuclear-tests-polynesia-declassified
- #183 https://www.theguardian.com/world/2008/nov/27/france-nuclear-tests-illness
- #180 http://www.stuff.co.nz/world/south-pacific/8872214/Mururoa-fallout-worse-than-first-thought
- #184 https://www.radionz.co.nz/international/pacific-news/307569/french-polynesia-goes-to-un-over-nuclear-compensation
- #185 #186 #187 https://www.radionz.co.nz/international/pacific-news/307804/the-battle-continues,-50-years-after-first-test-at-mururoa
- #188 http://www.stuff.co.nz/national/94208355/thirtytwo-years-after-the-rainbow-warrior-bombing-unapologetic-french-spy-christine-cabon-is-found

#162 General Directorate for External Security (French: Direction générale de la sécurité extérieure, DGSE) is France's external intelligence agency.

#163 https://nzhistory.govt.nz/people/ernest-rutherford

#164 https://asiasociety.org/education/brief-history-nuclear-weapons-states

#165 http://www.icanw.org/the-facts/catastrophic-harm/blast-heat-and-radiation/

#167 https://www.ucsusa.org/nuclear-power/cost-nuclear-power

#168 https://www.conserve-energy-future.com/pros-and-cons-of-nuclear-energy.php

#170 https://www.globalresearch.ca/new-book-concludes-chernobyl-death-toll-985-000-mostly-from-cancer/20908

#171 https://www.globalresearch.ca/fukushima-a-nuclear-war-without-a-war-the-unspoken-crisis-of-worldwide-nuclear-radiation/28870

#172 Helen Caldicott, *Fukushima: Nuclear Apologists Play Shoot the Messenger on Radiation*, The Age, April 26, 2011

#173 Weyler, Rex (6 October 2004). *Greenpeace: How a Group of Ecologists, Journalists, and Visionaries Changed the World*

#174 *Radioactive Heaven and Earth: The Health and Environmental Effects of Nuclear Weapons Testing In, On, and Above the Earth*. IPPNW, 1991, chapter 9.

#175 #177 #178 http://www.peaceportal.org/documents/129875579/130263921/FangataufaMururoa.pdf

#176 Stanley, David (1 January 2000). *South Pacific Handbook*. David Stanley. p. 262. ISBN 978-1-56691-172-6

#179 "NUCLEAIRE - Moruroa réclame 'le droit de savoir'". La Depeche (in French)

#181 http://www.nuclear-risks.org/en/hibakusha-worldwide/fangataufa-and-moruroa.html

#189 https://www.mfe.govt.nz/sites/default/files/clean-green-aug01-final.pdf

#194 Refer Desmond Tutu page 44

PHOTO CREDITS

EXTRAORDINARY WOMEN, THE STORY OF AOTEAROA/NEW ZEALAND WOMEN'S RIGHT TO VOTE:

Pg 9   Women voting in 1893
ATL Reference: PA1-o-550-34-1

Pg 19   Mary Wollstonecraft
John Opie-National Portrait Gallery (NPG) circa 1797 NPG 1237 www.npg.org.uk

Pg 11   Kate Edgar
© Nelson College for Girls

Pg 13   Kate Sheppard
ATL Reference: 1/2-C-09028 -F

Pg 14   Left   Original Petition
ATL Reference: EP-1993-2285 Dominion Post Collection PAColl-7327 Photograph by Melanie Burford

Pg 14   Right   Notice
ATL Reference: Eph-B-WOMEN-1902

Pg 16   Mary Ann Müller
ATL Reference: 1/2-021456

Pg 17   An Appeal   Cover of the original 1869 pamphlet, held at Hocken Library, Dunedin

Pg 18   New Zealand $10 note
The Reserve Bank of New Zealand

Pg 19   Newspaper Notice
Gospel Temperance Meeting, Christchurch City Libraries Reference: Lyttelton Times, 12 May1885

Pg 21   New Plymouth 1893
Puke Ariki - Taranaki Museum & Library Reference: PHO2008-626 Photograph by George H. White

Pg 22   Meri Te Tai Mangakāhia
Davis Collection, Auckland War Memorial Museum C5101

Pg 23   Wedding of Niniwa-i-te-rangi and Tamaihotua Aporo
ATL Ref: PAColl-3861-43-18 (records/23059660)

Pg 24   Henry Smith Fish
ATL Reference 35mm-00127-a-F (records/23029548)

Pg 25   Detail from Infographic: Human rights of women
Copyright © UN Women. United Nations Entity for Gender Equality and the Empowerment of Women http://www.unwomen.org/en/digital-library/multimedia/2015/12/infographic-human-rights-women

Pg 28   Suffragette March 1910
Suffragette city: New Zealand supporters of the British women's suffrage campaign march in London, 1910 Auckland Institute and Museum Library. https://www.nzedge.com/legends/kate-sheppard/

Pg 29   Lady voters 1899
Auckland Libraries Heritage Images Collection Classification 324.3 [1] Photo: Beattie and Sanderson

THE GREAT DIVIDE, 1981 SPRINGBOK TOUR:

Pg 32   Top   John Kirk
ATL Reference PAColl-7985-55
Middle   Robert Muldoon ATL Reference EP/1979/3050-F

Pg 32   Bottom   David Lange
Commons.wikimedia.org/wiki/File:David_Lange_Posts_a_Letter.jpg

Pg 33   A line of police during protests at the test against South Africa. 15 August 1981NZ Herald, Photographer Paul Estcourt. Image code: NZH-1027157

Pg 34   City of Durban Sign
Copyright free.

Pg 36   Apartheid Signage, 1953
Kliptown, Johannesburg, 1979. Part of the collection from Paul Weinberg *Then and Now* exhibition at Duke University. - Wikimedia Roadside sign. Copyright free.

Pg 37   Top   Park Bench
Children sit on bench in Durban, May 27, 1960. Copyright free.

Pg 37   Bottom   Sports crowd
The segregated stands of a sports arena in Bloemfontein, South Africa, 1 May 1969. UN Photo/H Vassal. www.unmultimedia.org/photo/

Pg 38   Poster: Ministry of Justice notice
https://digitalcollections.hoover.org/objects/31784

Pg 39	Top	Sign: Caution Beware of Natives
		Road Sign - 1956. © Hulton Archive
Pg 39	Bottom	Sign: For Use by Whites
		Racial Segregation: https://en.wikipedia.org/wiki/Apartheid
Pg 40		We Bleed the Same Colour
		Anti-Apartheid Graffiti. Copyright free.
Pg 41	Left	Soweto Uprising
		Getty images reference number 01296458
Pg 41	Right	Sharpville massacre
		South Africa Civil Rights. Copyright free.
Pg 42		Black Sash Protest
		https://allthatsinteresting.com/apartheid-south-africa
Pg 44		Citizens All Black Tour Association
		ATL Reference: Eph-D-RACIAL-1959-01
Pg 45		Anti-apartheid Group HART Protest
		Wellington Airport in 1971, Fairfax Media
Pg 46		Cartoon: Gleneagles
		ATL Reference: A-322-068 © Bromhead, 22 July 1981
Pg 49		Bob Walton Police Commissioner, copyright free.
		John Minto https://rdln.wordpress.com/2011/07/15/greater-even-than-rugby-the-1981-springbok-tour/
Pg 50		Rugby Park Hamilton Protest
		www.stuff.co.nz/sport/photos/2845036/Hamiltons-Rugby-Park-1981-Springboks-tour-protest Photographer John Selkirk
Pg 51	Top	Reverend George Armstrong
		ATL Reference EP/1981/2598/28A-F (records/22771129)
	Bottom	Third test at Eden Park, 1981
		ATL Reference: EP/1081/2657/9,
		Evening Post Collection (PAColl-0614)
		Photographer Don Scott
Pg 53	Left	Police and demonstrators clash
		Molesworth St, July 29, 1981. www.stuff.co.nz/dominion-post/capital-life/8998581
	Right	16 year old high school student
		Karen Brough www.stuff.co.nz/dominion-post/capital-life/8998581
Pg 55		Injured Protester, Wellington, 1981
		© The Dominion Post
Pg 56		Flour Bombing Eden Park
		Marx Jones flies over Eden Park, Auckland, https://www.nzgeo.com/stories/tainted-games/
Pg 57		Clowns - anti-Springbok tour demonstrators
		1981 Springbok tour NZHerald Image code: NZH-1059126
Pg 57		Aeroplane drops flour on All Blacks
		12 September 1981. NZ Herald Image code: NZH-1000624. Photographer Ross Land
Pg 58		Nelson Mandela Copyright free
		FW de Klerk and Nelson Mandela Copyright free
Pg 61	Top	Nelson Mandela Copyright free
	Left	Desmond Tutu ttps://en.wikipedia.org/wiki/Desmond_Tutu#/media/File:Archbishop-Tutu-medium.jpg
	Middle	Steve Biko
		https://en.wikipedia.org/w/index.php?curid=54095214, WP:NFCC#4
	Right	John Minto, NZ Herald
	Left	John Kirk, ATL Reference: PAColl-7985-55. Records/22885188
	Middle	Donna Awatere Copyright free
	Right	Trevor Richards Photographer. Bridget Williams Books.
	Left	Ripeka Evans
		With thanks to Massey University
	Middle	Syd Jackson
		https://en.wikipedia.org/w/index.php?curid=49623008, WP:NFCC#4
	Right	Will 'Ilolahia
		NZ Herald

RACISM NEVER SLEEPS, THE DAWN RAIDS:

Pg 63	Little Polynesia
	Still captured from Polynesian Panthers, Tumanako Productions, 2010. Courtesy of the stills Collection, New Zealand Film Archive Ngā Kaitiaki O Ngā Taonga Whitiāhua
Pg 67	March Against Racism, Wellington, October 2004
	Scoop Images: Multicultural Aotearoa In Wellington, Article: Alastair Thompson, Photo essay by Kevin List and Alastair Thompson
Pg 69	Sequence of screen grabs
	National Party 1975 Election TV Advertisement. You can see more of the ad on this link. https://www.newshub.co.nz/home/politics/2017/05/throwback-1970s-national-ad-warned-of-immigrations-affect-on-housing.html
Pg 72	Amnesty Aroha Poster
	from DOL 22/1/310 pt. 3. Ibid. Auckland Police Association, "Police Action Regarding Illegal Immigrants," Press Release, 25/10/76 in Police 1/1/27 v. 2. Lifted from: Immigration and National Identity in 1970s New Zealand by James Mitchell, A thesis submitted for the degree of Doctor of Philosophy at the University of Otago, July 2003 (https://docplayer.net/60257439-P-r-o-t-e-c-t-i-o-n-o-f-a-u-t-h-o-r-s-c-o-p-y-r-i-g-h-t.html)

Pg 74   Polynesian Panther Party Logo
        Copyright unknown
Pg 75   Left   Sweatshirt branding
        Copyright unknown'
        Right   Protest march
        Screen grab from 'Polynesian Panthers Documentary' https://www.nzonscreen.com/title/polynesian-panthers-2010
Pg 78   The Un-level Playing Field
        © Chris Slade
Pg 79   On Tolerance and Acceptance
        Sharon Murdoch © Stuff.co.nz
        Let's Unravel It
        Sharon Murdoch © Stuff.co.nz
Pg 80   The Dawn Raids - Educate to Liberate, exhibition. © John Miller - George Jackson/ Soledad Brothers solidarity march to the U.S. Consulate on Queen Street, 3 March 1972.

SHIPS, SPIES & SABOTAGE, THE BOMBING OF THE RAINBOW WARRIOR:

Pg 83   The Rainbow Warrior hull
        The Greenpeace flagship Rainbow Warrior, 01 August 1985. Photo: AFP
Pg 85   Top   Fernando Pereira with his daughter. Image sourced from the https://www.greenpeace.org/new-zealand/about/our-history/bombing-of-the-rainbow-warrior/the-bombing-of-the-rainbow-warrior-fact-file/
        Bottom   The Rainbow Warrior submerged
        With thanks to Greenpeace
Pg 86   Top   The Rainbow Warrior
        Herald picture / Ben Motu
        Newspaper Articles
        Reports from The New Zealand Herald
        Bottom   The Rainbow Warrior hull
        Image sourced with thanks to Greenpeace
Pg 87   Newspaper Article
        Report from The New Zealand Herald
        The Rainbow Warrior wheelhouse
        Photo: NZ Herald
Pg 88   Divers working on the Rainbow Warrior
        Image taken from the news item '30 years on, French agent apologises for sinking Rainbow Warrior'
        https://www.france24.com/en/20150906-france-rainbow-warrior-dgse-sinking-greenpeace

Pg 91   French Bomber Christine Cabon
        Photo Ascension Torrent
Pg 92   Left   Hiroshima Aftermath, cropped version with writing of Paul Tibbets. Date: shortly after 6 August 1945
        https://en.wikipedia.org/wiki/File:Hiroshima_aftermath.jpg
        Right   The Genbaku Dome
        A view of the damaged Hiroshima Prefecture Industrial Promotion Hall, now called The Genbaku Dome amidst the devastation in October 1945. Image taken from: http://hiroshima.australiandoctor.com.au/
Pg 93   Top   Scars left from radiation bur
        Image taken from: http://hiroshima.australiandoctor.com.au
        Left   Direct, thermal flash burns
        National Museum of Health and Medicine / Science Photo Library
        Right   Hiroshima survivers
        Public domain image. https://en.wikipedia.org/wiki/File:Hiroshima_Street_Scene_with_injured_Civilians.jpg
Pg 96   Left   New Zealand Stamp
        Credit: New Zealand Post
        Right   Protest French nuclear testing
        ATL Reference: 1/4-020364-F / URL: https://nzhistory.govt.nz/media/photo/protest-against-french-nuclear-testing, (Ministry for Culture and Heritage), updated 20-Dec-2012
        Bottom   Matiu Rata
        ATL Evening Post collection, Reference Number PAColl-0614-1 Photographer: The Evening Post
Pg 97   Norman Kirk
        ATL Reference: PAColl-7985-55
        CANWAR   ATL "The Dominion Post Collection" Reference: EP/1976/2841/26a-F
Pg 98   David Lange
        Credit: Stuff.co.nz. https://www.stuff.co.nz/national/politics/opinion/88322605/karl-du-fresne-lange-not-all-that-he-seemed
Pg 101 Wreck of the Rainbow Warrior
        Credit: Photographer © Ian Skipworth

Pg 103 French base on Moruroa Atoll.
Credit: Photographer © Greenpeace/Daniel Beltrá.
A nuclear bomb Detonated by the French government at the Mururoa atoll, French Polynesia. Credit: J. Pierre / FLICKR

Pg 104 Moruroa Location map - Copyright free
Moruroa (Mururoa, Mururura)
This work has been released into the public domain by its author, Peter Minton.

Pg 105 Left   Jean Luc Kister
Photo: TVNZ
Right   Christine Cabon
Credit: Ascension Torrent: Stuff.co.nz.
Cecile Meier and Kelly Dennett

Pg 107 Rainbow Warrior (1955), Auckland, NZ
Wikimedia Commons: File:RainbowWarrior-1985b.jpg.

ADVICE FOR RESEARCHING IN A 'FAKE NEWS' WORLD:

1 Polish up your critical thinking

Many sites producing or reproducing fake news or 'spin' are written in a provocative way to get 'clicks' on that site. Their goal is to make their information believable, so people will read and disseminate the information because they believe it is true. This means taking extra care to check material using the tools below. But first and foremost, enter research with a critical eye and don't take it 'face value'. These sites are designed to provoke people at an emotional level so they accept the information without question.

Always ask yourself:
- What is the motive? Why has this been written?
- Is it trying to persuade me to believe a certain viewpoint?
- Is it trying to sell me a product or idea?
- If there are links to follow, are they credible?
- Why do they want me to click through?

2 Check the source

Dig, dig, dig! When you come across a source you've never heard of you need to go digging! Is it coming from some reputable news agency or research facility (not funded by interest groups) or is it from a personal blog? As a general rule, you should always have at least two reputable sources for a story before you do anything with it.

Mindtools.com suggests you 'check the URL of the Pg, too. (A URL, or Uniform Resource Locator, is a web address that helps browsers to find a site on the internet.) Strange-sounding URLs that end in extensions like ".infonet" and ".offer," rather than ".com" or ".co.uk," or that contain spelling errors, may mean that the source is suspect.'

Pay special attention to the domain: often, students will use .edu, .gov, .com or .org sites for research, as they are fact checked and have good oversight. When in doubt, click the site's home Pg and investigate who they are from there.

When the information comes directly from someone, ask yourself whether this is their area of expertise? Are they known for giving well-sourced information? Have they ever been known to exaggerate or skew the truth for their own ends?

You can test whether something is 'fake' by checking it on www.snopes.com or FactCheck.org or PolitiFact.com.

3 Check to see who else is reporting this story
Have other reputable news sources reported this story? The large news organisations have fact-checkers and verify their information before they publish it. Check whether the story has been picked up by other well-known news producers. Stories that appear nowhere else should be treated with suspicion. Try Radio New Zealand https://www.rnz.co.nz/news, Newsroom https://www.newsroom.co.nz/, our main television news and newspapers — however, remember that all information is filtered through the journalist presenting the information, so even our major news outlets should be questioned for bias and unsourced speculation.

Be careful you have actually found the official site. Sometimes fake websites pretend to be official sites — and have been known to edit images and mock-up newspaper articles to make them look official when they're not. If a website has published fake news before, there's a good chance they'll do it again.

Check the date to make sure it's current. A lot of false news are simply old stories being presented as new events.

4 Thoroughly examine the evidence
A trustworthy news story will contain lots of facts you can check, such as quotes from experts, survey data and official statistics. If there is no supporting evidence, and/or the source comes from an unknown or discredited expert or someone's 'friend,' then question it.

Does the evidence prove that something definitely happened? Or have the facts been 'spun' to support a particular point of view?
If you can't independently verify an article, especially if it makes extravagant claims, it's best to stay away from it. With genuine news, reporters are constantly working to verify and check what others are reporting on, much the same way scientists validate the work of other scientists.

5 Look for Fake Images
These days it's easy to use editing software to create fake images that look real and professional. Be very wary. Research coming from Cornell University shows that only half of research subjects could tell when images are fake.

There are, however, some warning signs you can watch out for. Mindtools.com warns of 'strange shadows on the image, or jagged edges around a figure.' If you're not sure, try using tools such as Google Reverse Image Search https://support.google.com/websearch/answer/1325808?hl=en to check whether the image has been changed or used out of context.

6 Check that it 'sounds right'
Finally, it's important that you always use your common sense! If a story sounds unbelievable, it probably is. But be on the lookout for fake news that is designed to feed your biases or fears. Just because a story sounds 'right' and true, doesn't mean it is.

Also keep in mind that some sites intentionally play around with the news as a form of satire. Examples might include The Onion or The Daily Mash.

If you do have doubts about a piece of information, or you know it's fake, avoid sharing it. Others may not be as rigorous at fact checking as you.

For a comprehensive guide, see Media Literacy And Fake News by Kerry Gallagher, J.D. and Larry Magid, Ed.D. https://www.connectsafely.org/wp-content/uploads/Media-Literacy-Fake-News.pdf

KEYWORDS

Facts: High-quality news should focus on the indisputable information needed to relay events. This includes the people involved, the places where it happened, and any additional important details and evidence.

Opinion: An important part of the news involves an individual's interpretation of the meaning or impact of an event or facts. Opinion can be a specific point of view or can be meant to convince others, as long as it is clearly labelled as opinion.

Source: https://www.connectsafely.org/wp-content/uploads/Media-Literacy-Fake-News.pdf

ACKNOWLEDGMENTS:

I'd particularly like to thank Redmer Yska, James Mitchell, Greenpeace NZ and the Union of Concerned Scientists (USA) for their generous permissions to quote extensively from their work.

I'd also like to acknowledge the excellent coverage available at Te Ara: the Encyclopedia of New Zealand and the New Zealand History website (Ministry for Culture and Heritage.)

Wherever possible I have referenced where the information has been sourced and attempted to contact individuals for their permission to quote. In some cases I have not received replies or have been unable to find a specific contact. Please accept my thanks and appreciation of your work. If you have concerns, please do contact me and I will make all attempts to rectify them.

I'd also like to thank Jenny Nagle and Christine Dale from OneTree House, for giving me this opportunity. I have found it an immensely interesting and enlightening project.

Mandy Hager